The Auth

Giancarlo Rinaldi was born, brought up and educated in Du[illegible]. He has an honours degree in Italian and French from the University of Edinburgh and has worked as a journalist for the *Dumfries and Galloway Standard* for ten years. He has written two previous books: *The Football Italia Season Guide 1993/94* and *From the Serchio to the Solway*. A committed Doonhamer, Rinaldi lives in the town with his wife and daughter.

To Chris & Ian,
Wishing you a very
Happy Christmas &
wonderful 2007.
Thinking of you —
Loads of love
Chris & Mary xx

GREAT DUMFRIES STORIES

Giancarlo Rinaldi

FORT PUBLISHING LTD

First published in 2005 by Fort Publishing Ltd, Old Belmont House,
12 Robsland Avenue, Ayr, KA7 2RW

Cover photograph by Duncan I. McEwan

Other photographs courtesy of Dumfries and Galloway, Libraries, Information and Archives unless otherwise stated

Typeset by Senga Fairgrieve (0131-658-1763)

Graphic design by Mark Blackadder

Printed by Bell and Bain Ltd, Glasgow

ISBN 0-9547431-2-1

To Mia

Hai illuminato la mia vita

CONTENTS

ACKNOWLEDGEMENTS

There are many people to thank in helping to put this book together. My sincere gratitude, in no particular order, to James McCarroll for approaching me with the idea and helping get it through to publication. To everybody at the *Standard* for their support and ideas – particularly that old head with so much local knowledge, Doug Archibald. Thanks also to another veteran reporter of the Dumfries scene, Bert Houston, for his advice and assistance. To Angela McIntosh at Dumfries police for a major steer in the right direction on those 'Deadly Doonhamers'. My movie experts, film officers past and present, Belle Doyle and Kenny Eggo (apologies Kenny for making it sound like you worked hard – I'll hear from your solicitors). To all the previous reporters of the *Dumfries and Galloway Standard* and other local publications for marking the town's history and also the local scribes and historians whose works I used to help guide me and inspire. A special thank you to everybody at the Ewart library – who put up with my excessive use of the photocopier and microfiche – especially Alice Brotherston who was so helpful with final queries. And an extra mention for Graham Roberts who provided enough help in one day to write three books and then had the dedication to help proof read. Finally to my wife Anne – always my first editor, agent and research assistant.

G. R.
Dumfries
March 2005

INTRODUCTION

A lot of people do not even know where Dumfries is. There is a belief, especially south of the border, that its name is part of a conspiracy to confuse outsiders. Dumfries, Dumbarton, Dunfermline, Dundee – who can really keep a track on which one is where? Blank looks are often the response when you tell a stranger the name of the town you hail from.

In the end, we usually settle on describing it as the first town across the border. This, of course, is not strictly true and would certainly depend upon the point where you crossed from England into Scotland. Nonetheless, we take a certain pride in being a frontier town, marking a major dividing line with its long and bloody history. Just listening to the way people talk in Carlisle and comparing it to Dumfries you know that there are some fairly significant differences.

Make no mistake, Dumfries definitely has its own special qualities – although that can be easy to forget. It is certainly more straightforward to focus on things it lacks, rather than what it has to offer. Indeed, many Doonhamers were dumbstruck when a survey suggested it was the best place to live in Britain back in 1997. 'Number One' trumpeted the newspapers as an eight-year survey looking at crime levels, employment, education and a range of other facilities across some two hundred towns and cities came up with the answer that Dumfries was the best of all. The researchers from Strathclyde University were convinced they had got it right but many locals were more than a little sheepish about the claims. Although they were quietly proud of their town, was it really the best place to live in Great Britain? Most had their doubts and if called upon to justify why their home was best would probably have struggled to come up with an answer.

Maybe that is because it is hard to pin down what marks out the Queen of the South as different from the rest of Scotland. We are close to England, but we are not English. We are at the heart of a rural community, but with some serious urban issues. We are proud of the achievements of our sons and daughters, but will shoot down anyone who gets too big for their boots. Try stuffing those contradictions into one easy definition.

The one thing we do share, however, is a common history – although that is something we often lose sight of. Sometimes we look back centuries in search of our shared heritage and then it slips from our grasp. Instead, there are many more modern moments which link us all together. The chances for the Dumfries community to revel in that fact are few and far between. Guid Nychburris, perhaps, or a sunshine Saturday at Dumfries show. Maybe even a glory moment or two at Palmerston park.

It might seem strange to say but perhaps the most inspiring sense of belonging comes only by travelling away from the town. Some of my own proudest moments to say I was from Dumfries have come on trips to two Challenge Cup finals following Queen of the South or on an away day to Easter Road in the League Cup. So, Motherwell, Clyde and Edinburgh are the places where I have been most keenly aware of what it means to come from Dumfries.

This book would love to tap into, and capture, some of the sentimental and emotional energy of those times when it felt special to be a Doonhamer. It is not meant to chart the history of the town in detail from the Middle Ages to the present day. Instead, the aim is simply to share a few stories from my own memories and research into the past century or so.

That has been a truly intriguing process for me. Although I was born and brought up in the town there are plenty of things I did not know. Walking along the High Street there is a tendency to keep your hands in your pockets and your eyes down. Look up for a moment and you will be surprised at the dates and names on the buildings around you and the stories they have to tell. This is a town that has seen plenty over the years.

Maybe these tales can bring back memories for local readers but also give outsiders an insight into what makes Doonhamers the way we are. The subjects have been deliberately limited to the last century or so in order to keep them relevant to Dumfries today. Most of the landmarks or buildings mentioned still stand and many of the people are still alive. History, after all, is not just about events that happened so many centuries ago that not even your great-great-great grandparents could have been involved.

Dumfries is a town that has known great changes over the last 100 years and some moments of great transformation. Whole industries have started while others have disappeared, the town centre has been revamped with the removal of traffic, a University campus has been born on a site where a mental asylum stood and countless other events of more or less significance have shaped our collective story.

I would neither claim to know every tale there is to tell about Dumfries nor to be the best teller of them. So take this book for what it is – a very personal view of some of the most memorable moments in the recent history of our town. There was not room to include everything I would have liked and the pressures of time always mean that a few tales will slip through your hands. Still, I hope there are enough entertaining stories here to keep anyone who holds the town dear happy. It may not be the greatest place in Britain to live but we love it just the same. Here's to Dumfries.

1

A RIVER RUNS THROUGH IT

Dumfries is a divided town. The river Nith runs right through its heart, splitting it in two. The boundary is now merely symbolic but it was not so long ago that crossing a bridge over the water meant stepping from one distinct community into another. Throughout the history of the town its river has played a key role. Bridges have been built across it, boats have sailed up it and both entertainment and industry have exploited its fast tidal flow. Modern times may have seen its commercial significance fade but it remains a very prominent symbol.

The Nith has always been important to Dumfries and still is. It has been the source of historical division, known more than its share of tragedy and become the site of regular disputes over how to improve the scenic qualities of the town. No story of Dumfries can be told without its river running through it.

The waters played a major dividing role until relatively recently. The 'unification' of the old burghs of Dumfries and Maxwelltown did not take place until 1929. Until then they had lived in a love-hate relationship with plenty of conflict between residents on either side of Devorgilla bridge. Some of this animosity was slow to die and old Maxwelltonians continued to lament the move up to the 1960s.

Fears were rife in the 1920s that the two communities on opposite sides of the Nith might lose their right to local autonomy. Moves were afoot at national level to remove the recognition of authorities with less than a 20,000 population. Both Dumfries and

Maxwelltown feared being swallowed up by a county council and it pushed them closer together. By 1927 a detailed report outlined the key points of amalgamation. Nothing was left to chance with arrangements made to cover rates, policing, common-good funds, fire brigade, licensing matters and even the £2,000 gifted by Miss McKie in 1897 for the purpose of providing baths and wash houses for the two burghs.

Clearly, there were some reservations on both sides of the river about joining forces. In Maxwelltown there was a fear that they would simply be swallowed up by their neighbour. While in Dumfries there was obviously a school of thought that it would prove costly for them in the long run to be saddled with their 'little brother' across the water as they might see a rise in rates. When the two provosts put forward the proposal in 1927 they were desperately keen to allay those fears. Provost O'Brien of Dumfries was determined not to give the impression it was a takeover bid:

> I think it right to state quite clearly that what the Dumfries Council desire to consider along with the Maxwelltown Council is not the absorption of Maxwelltown by Dumfries or the extension of Dumfries, but to try to work out whether for the mutual benefit of both burghs it would not be better that there should be a united administration. . . . The matter of the independence and identity of burghs is one which should not be lightly interfered with. There was a time not so very long ago when Dumfries inhabitants and Maxwelltown inhabitants were separate peoples, each having a separate identity and, in a gradually diminishing sense, a separate mode of life.

There was similar caution from his Maxwelltown counterpart, provost Brodie, who was anxious not to be seen to be speaking too strongly in favour of the plans. He also clearly spelt out the matters that his residents would not tolerate:

> Provost O'Brien wisely disclaims any intention or desire on the part of Dumfries to absorb Maxwelltown, and that is so far good. A proposal which involved the wiping out of our identity and the shedding of our independence by simply merging Maxwelltown with Dumfries is not likely to be received with universal favour . . . I have always recognised that the aims and interests of the two burghs are virtually one, and, that, but for the position of the river Nith, would always have been one.

The proposals made enough sense to both communities for them to progress – albeit not without some difficulty – to a full agreement within the space of a couple of years. The *Dumfries and Galloway Standard's* editorial comment came down in favour of the plans: 'There is a gratifying absence of the spirit of jealousy and hostility that has often marked a movement for unification of control in other places,' it commented. 'When amalgamation does take place it will not be by one burgh or the other being defeated. . . . They will agree to unite as partners, not indeed equal in historical prestige or in population, but in other respects on an equal footing.'

And so the big day for hands across the river Nith came in October 1929. The celebration was declared a general holiday and the main events took place at St Michael's bridge where the Duke of Buccleuch opened a ceremonial gate to signify the end to barriers between the two burghs. This allowed Maxwelltown town councillors to stride confidently into Dumfries to take their place with their 'brothers' from across the water. The day ended, fittingly enough, on the banks of the Nith with fireworks at the Mill Green.

Estimates put the crowd at around ten thousand for the historic day and the weather was reported as favourable, although there was a cold wind. Clearly no expense was spared on the banquet at the assembly rooms, which was reckoned to be the most sizeable in the town since the Burns centenary feast of 1896. If the menu is anything to go by the 300 diners certainly ate their fill. In the space of one and three-quarter hours they munched their way through 100 loaves, 1,150 assorted hors d'oeuvres, 12 gallons of soup, 300 fillets of sole, 40 chickens, 100 pounds of roast sirloin, 2 hundred-weights of potatoes, 56 pounds of cauliflower, 56 pounds of peas and a hundredweight of Messrs Oughton's special Queen of the South pudding! Also polished off were 300 dinner rolls, 400 sand-wiches, 400 cakes, half-a-hundredweight of sugar, three gallons of coffee and five gallons of milk. Clearly amalgamation was not a thing to be done on an empty stomach.

The Duke of Buccleuch summed up the feelings of those present rather neatly with his words at the ceremonial unification: 'an interesting speech, given forth in virile tones' said the reporter of the day. And he recognised the important part the Nith had to play in proceedings.

> For many years the only division between the two communities has been our beautiful Nith. That has been a barrier between you, but everyone must see that it was not so intended. What town is not the more beautiful for a lovely river running through it? And it is as certain as we are here today that providence did not design the Nith to be a barrier, but, on the contrary, to be a bond of union. . . . The Provost has told you that there have been ups and downs during the last fifty years or more between the two burghs and as regards their amalgamation. Is it not very much the same as happens with human beings? There are very often ups and downs. There is sometimes a good deal of hesitation but that does not prevent the eventual union taking place at last . . . I might say Providence must have its way and today we are able to see the gallant of Maxwelltown clasped in the loving arms of the Queen of the South.

The move brought to an end more than seventy years of 'courtship' between the two sides. Two previous votes on the proposals had been defeated, one overwhelmingly in 1927. But, a year later, the fear that new legislation would leave Dumfries without any local government powers turned a majority against amalgamation of more than 700 into a majority in favour among local ratepayers of 763. And so Dumfries had its day of celebration on the banks of the Nith.

The river has not always enjoyed such happy times. It is in the nature of currents that they can claim lives and over the years the Nith has had its share of tragedy. One particularly poignant disaster happened just a year before amalgamation, in 1928. Robert Irving lost his life attempting to save his 3-year-old son who had fallen into the river.

The young father had gone out to search for his two sons at about five o'clock on a Saturday afternoon. He tracked down one of them but wandered along to the Mill Green only to spot his youngest son, William, being carried away by the current. Despite being unable to swim he threw himself into the waters in an attempt to rescue the boy.

Another man arrived on the scene and tried to find the life-saving gear kept at the Mill Green but could not locate it. There seems little doubt that if the gear had been available then disaster could have been avoided. Instead, William Kirkpatrick, a bookbinder, rushed from his home in Millbrae Terrace on hearing that a child had fallen into the water. When he got there he got more than he bargained for as he tried to save the boy. 'While he was struggling in the water he was surprised to find after he had got a grip of the child that there was also a man in the water in danger of drowning,' said one report of the time. 'Kirkpatrick made a very heroic endeavour to effect a double rescue, but his strength was unequal to the heavy demands made upon it.'

In the meantime another man – a telephone linesman named William Smith, from Welldale Terrace – tried to help Kirkpatrick out. He had been watching a man fishing when he heard the cries for help. He dashed to the scene and entered the waters just as Kirkpatrick was flopping, exhausted, on the shore. After fighting with the fast-flowing river for some time he was helped onto dry land along with the boy, but it appears that there was confusion when he told people on the bank there was still a man to be rescued, as a newspaper report made clear:

> Smith was assured that the man who had been in the water had already struggled ashore, and Kirkpatrick, who was standing some distance away with water dripping from his clothes, was pointed out to him. Smith persisted in his contention that there was still a man in the water and it was only with difficulty that those on the banking were able to restrain him from again entering the flooded river. The hopelessness of the situation was evident in view of the state of the river.

The boy, after some medical attention, was reported to be making good progress. But the body of his father was washed away – he had met a tragic end trying to rescue his little son, despite the attempts of two valiant rescuers.

A similar disaster had struck at Kingholm quay just a short distance downstream a few years earlier. Once again it was a family catastrophe as the Nith claimed the lives of two brothers. Joseph, Charles and James Langton had gone out to play near the harbourmaster's boat on a Thursday afternoon in January 1922. They were within fifty yards of their own front door when tragedy struck.

Details of what exactly happened to the three pupils of St Andrew's primary school are unclear but it was thought that the youngest, Joseph, aged five, had been pulling the rope of the harbourmaster's boat when he got dragged into the water. On seeing this, his oldest brother, James, jumped in to save him. The result – with the river Nith at full flow – was disaster. Charles ran home to tell them what had happened but by the time rescuers reached the scene Joseph's body was already floating in the water. The body of his brother was recovered a few hours later.

Thankfully, such tragedies have become far fewer in more recent times and the focus of attention has been on restoring the Nith to its former glory as a centrepiece for the town. Much money has been spent on improving the riverbank walks while constant cries are made for a clean-up operation to drag the worst of the debris from the waters.

In the mid-1990s more than £1.2 million was spent on 'environmental improvements' at the Whitesands. Regional councillors and the enterprise company set aside £500,000 for the plans and secured European funding to complete the work. Much of the development involved landscaping the area, putting in new seating and improving walkways. What the money could not address, however, was the public's wish for a flood-prevention scheme, a new bus station and commercial development. Nonetheless, the completed works did constitute a major investment in the riverbank area.

Less successful, at least judging by stories in the media, were attempts to clean up the river and in the autumn of 2003 the restoration of the area was once again top of the local news agenda. Traders and councillors were united in their calls for closer attention to be given to the area. Their biggest gripe was the level of overgrown weed on the riverbanks, which would play against any ambitions the town might have to use the Nith as a magnet for tourists. Litter also remained a problem and one reader of the *Standard* even suggested the area was so filthy that it should be renamed the Blacksands. Still, a meeting of delegates from business, council and other bodies agreed to make the area a top priority. And they found funding to back up their aims the following year.

In February 2004 a pot of £26,000 was found to clear up the river after the regular complaints about litter and the overgrown weeds and scrub. The section between the swimming pool and the Dock park was given top priority for rubbish removal as well as plans to dispose of trees and shrubs that had started to look particularly unsightly as they sprouted through retaining walls. But one part of the clean-up plans had to be ditched because of environmental concerns. It had been hoped that the reeds around the Whitesands toilets could be removed but the Scottish Environment Protection Agency vetoed these proposals since the area had become a natural habitat for wildlife. In some ways the neglect of the area had now become its salvation. A spokesman for the council explained: 'SEPA's concern is with pollution to the river but it also has an additional role concerning bio-diversity of the river such as wildlife and insect life. It had no problems with us cutting trees and shrubs that have come through the walls and similarly has no problems with a litter pick-up.' So, at least some cosmetic changes could take place in the area.

The clean-up was a definite boost as were ambitious plans announced in the spring of 2004 to develop a new arts and culture centre for the town. It was hoped that multi-million pound plans could create a new 'hub' for the arts focussing on the Ewart library and a Whitesands site. The proposal for the riverside was to replace the Robert Burns centre on the Maxwelltown side of the river with a new cinema-based attraction possibly on the other bank. Councillors were again keen to promote the area to visitors and locals alike and help its regeneration. Also on the cards was the closure of the ailing swimming pool on the banks of the Nith, which had been state of the art in the 1960s but by the start of the twenty-first century was suffering a number of problems and urgently needed to be replaced. Once again, the local authority had agreed a preferred site on the old Co-op land on Leafield Road. All of which would mean a radical new look for the Whitesands, which have for so long been a vital cog in the history of Dumfries, and there is no doubt that the banks of the river Nith will play a key part in the regeneration of the town.

2

THAT'S ENTERTAINMENT

Not many world tours stop off in Dumfries. By and large the big bands do not gig here, the major theatre companies do not perform and the top films often take weeks to reach local screens. This has not always been the case, however, as at times in its history some of the most dazzling shows of the day have stopped in the town.

Imagine the excitement in Victorian Dumfries when Barnum and Bailey arrived with their spectacular show in October 1899. It was the last leg of their Scottish tour and clearly went down a treat. An amazing 14,000 people crammed under their tent at Cresswell to see the performance. By comparison, that is more than double the crowd that packed Palmerston to see Queen of the South win promotion from the second division in 2002.

Special trains chugged into town from outlying villages to see the show, the organisation of which must have been something of a military operation in itself. It required four trains to carry the equipment, animals and performers, which meant that a total of seventy-four carriages eventually pulled into the Lockerbie Road goods station. And to publicise the event, as if it was necessary, many of the circus animals were paraded along St Michael Street, Whitesands, Buccleuch Street, High Street, English Street and Leafield Road. Among the creatures strolling through the town centre were camels, zebras, hyenas, leopards, lions, tigers and even a herd of sixteen elephants.

Naturally the excitement this provoked led to huge crowds flocking to the performance at the enormous tent, which was 600 feet long by 240 feet wide. Cresswell Avenue was blocked by the large crowds who wanted to see the dubious attractions on offer. These included an eight-foot-tall Egyptian beside a twenty-two-inch-high 'Hindoo woman' and, of course, the obligatory bearded lady. And the spectacular trapeze and horse-riding acts were particularly popular.

The town was treated to a similar spectacle just five years later in Cresswell Park. 'For One Day Only', announced the advert, there was the opportunity to see one of the most exciting shows in the world: 'Buffalo Bill's Wild West and Congress of Rough Riders of the World headed and personally introduced by Col W. F. Cody – Buffalo Bill'.

The excitement was intense as the build-up to the big day in September 1904 gathered momentum. 'It is almost futile to attempt to enumerate all the interesting features of the great Wild West show, which is shortly to be seen here,' commented the *Dumfries and Galloway Standard* of the time – before going on to do precisely that. Among the attractions of the show were Cossacks, gauchos and many other noted horsemen from around the globe. The colonel was met at the Coffee House hotel (located at 110 High Street, a site now occupied by Burton's) on his arrival in Dumfries and Mr Dickson, English Street, was ready to sell packets of 'beautiful mementoes' of the event.

Buffalo Bill put on two shows – one in the afternoon and the other in the evening – on land next to Cresswell House. Despite being late in arriving from Stranraer the first performance went ahead as planned and 12,000 spectators are reported to have attended. 'At the day-performance all parts of the house were crowded with the exception of a portion of that reserved for holders of three shilling and two shilling tickets,' one reporter commented. 'The assemblage was a motley but highly picturesque one, typical of many nationalities and many phases of life, some of them now little more than historic memories although the actual participants in them stood before us.'

And what did Doonhamers make of the great man? Bill Cody clearly made quite an impression, according to one observer:

> He is a lithe veteran of fifty-eight with flowing hair and a bearing suggestive of the old cavalier type. He has come through much tough work as a scout and a soldier in the frontier wars with the Indians, and has for the last twenty-two years of his life been touring the world with the exhibition that illustrates some of the scenes amid which his earlier career was passed.

Buffalo Bill had an inspirational, and highly complimentary, speech for the assembled multitude:

> I am very proud to be here in this ancient and historical city of Dumfries. When I was a younger man the greater part of my life was spent on the border lands between Indian savagery and civilisation. Speaking in Dumfries, that stood so long as the border city between England and Scotland in the days of the Bruces, when wars ravaged the country, I feel that I am addressing the descendants of a people who, like myself, were in the thickest of the fray. . . . In your Robert Burns, who made the whole world kin, is another link between America and Scotland, for he is the world's poet, and America claims a share. Dumfries being our last place visited in Scotland, it will ever be recalled as the first.

This was proof, if it were needed, that American entertainers have always known how to get on the right side of crowds on this side of the pond.

The performances seem to have gone without a hitch although the use of electric light for the evening display reduced the quality of vision for Doonhamers and the many folk who travelled in from outlying areas. In between performances Cody invited members of the local medal-presentation committee back to his room for a drink. 'He is himself an abstainer but proffered his hospitality with the remark that if his guests chose to drink poison it was no concern of his.' How many took a drink offered in such a manner is not recorded. Overall, however, Dumfries enjoyed its brush with the Wild West.

The years up to the Second World War were characterised by simpler pleasures if the entertainments of the day are anything to go by. There was, for example, the popular pursuit of roller skating on a rink in the drill hall in the early 1900s. And in the 1930s a crowd of 1,500 was drawn to the opening of the greyhound stadium at Essex Park in Noblehill. The appropriately named Mr Wolffe brought the sport to the town with six races: four for greyhounds and two for whippets and there was 'considerable speculation on the totalisator' with 'several well known dogs taking part'.

One form of entertainment that quickly captured the imagination was the cinema. Even from the pioneering days of the silent movies Dumfries was passionate about the silver screen. The first viewings were at the Lyceum in the High Street, at the 'Electric Theatre' in the Theatre Royal and at the Mechanics Theatre in Irish Street. But the real boom happened in the 1930s.

In 1931 Dumfries was treated to the arrival of the Regal cinema, which boasted around 1,700 seats on its site at the end of Shakespeare Street. Five years later, in 1936, a new Lyceum was built on the old site in High Street, and the movies on that opening night included *The Littlest Rebel* starring Shirley Temple. On opening the new cinema the chairman of directors, Mr M. H. McKerrow, said: 'The Lyceum is primarily a cinema but care has been taken to have it fully equipped for the production of all kinds of dramatic art, so when an opportunity occurs the Lyceum can offer accommodation equal to many London theatres.'

These were the golden years of cinema with the picture palaces thriving right through the war years and into the 1950s, with live shows also attracting big crowds to the large Lyceum stage. But the advent of television hit the cinemas and theatres hard.

And so it was a predictable, yet sad, moment when the Lyceum was demolished in September 1969. During its illustrious history it had hosted some of the country's most famous comedians, including the likes of Dave Willis (best known for his rendition of 'My Wee Gas Mask'), Will Fyffe (of 'I Belong To Glasgow' fame) and Sir Harry Lauder as well as internationally renowned musicians like Alfredo Campoli. It was very much a sign of the times when the Dean of Guild Court (which met in the municipal chambers in Buccleuch Street and operated like today's planning committee) granted a warrant for properties in the High Street, including the picture house, to be knocked down. In their place, plans for a supermarket and 'five lock-up shops' were approved. 'The new development will form part of the pedestrian precinct conception for the lower part of the High Street' reported the *Standard*. 'But Dumfries which once could boast three busy picture houses, will now have only one.'

The Regal also had to move with the times and, in 1972, it was split into two to accommodate a bingo hall and renamed the ABC. It became a Cannon cinema in the 1990s and was the only sizeable local screen. Later it switched again to become the Odeon. Fans with a taste for art-house productions were catered for in the cosy atmosphere of the Robert Burns centre's film theatre, which was opened in 1986 by Princess Alexandra. Still, by the twenty-first century, Doonhamers in search of a good movie were sorely underprovided for and calls for a multi-screen cinema persisted every time a major leisure complex was proposed for the town.

If cinema has had its ups and downs it was the same story for the music and café culture of the 1950s. The rock and roll era saw many coffee shops, complete with jukebox, open for business and they were invariably run by Italians. It was impossible to walk from one end of the town to the other without passing a café: they included Dante's, Pioli's, Matthew's, the CR café, the College café and many more.

By the 1960s music was at the top of every teenager's agenda and some well-known groups came to town. But there was also a minor music revolution in Dumfries in early 1964. Around a thousand teenagers packed into the Drill Hall to see no fewer than nine bands battle it out in a 'beat competition'. It was dubbed the Solway Sound by organiser Jimmy Fisher and brought in contenders from across Dumfries and Galloway. From Dumfries came some cracking names like The Orbits, The Vulcans, The Interns, The Sekrets and The Roadrunners while 'invading' from out of town came The Black Knights from Kirkconnel, The Jaguars from Kirkcudbright, The Future Men from Castle Douglas and The Cherokees all the way from Stranraer. It was this last group – whose members dressed like Native Americans complete with headdress – that stole the show. Overall the concert lasted five hours but the newspapers reported that it went off without a hitch, despite the fears expressed in some quarters. One paper commented: 'The exemplary way in which the youngsters conducted themselves finally nailed the lie about Dumfries' alleged loutish, drunken and rowdy teenagers'. The event was a resounding success but as the decade went on the Solway Sound started to fade as the days of every town and village having at least one band to its name started to disappear. Indeed today it appears that the best the town can hope for in musical terms are appearances by stars of the 1980s attempting to revive their careers or by an up-and-coming, but unknown, local act.

However, when it comes to entertainment in Dumfries, one event stands out from the rest. The 'Rood' Fair has been an institution in the town for centuries and usually heralds the arrival of heavy September rains. The town had the right to hold three annual fairs: in February (which was mainly a horse fair), in July and the Rood in September, the most popular of the three fairs.

The name is said to be derived from the discovery by the Empress Helena of the cross on which Christ was crucified. The ancient relic was put on show in Jerusalem on 14 September, in AD 335, and was thereafter celebrated on that day by Greek and Latin churches. Many churches were dedicated to the Holy Rood, or cross, and the observance of the day continued throughout the Middle Ages. Dumfries adapted the timing to fit in between that date and the feast day of its own patron saint, Michael the Archangel, which fell on 29 September.

The popularity of the event can be seen by the fact that in the 1830s as many as 6,000 head of cattle went on sale. The day was also the occasion for the hiring of farm servants, which took place on the Whitesands or on the High Street close to the old *Standard* office on the Wednesday of Rood Fair week. But as the agricultural element faded so the emphasis on entertainment grew. At the turn of the nineteenth century the *Gallovidian* magazine commented on its transformation from a religious event into one devoted to pleasure.

> If the 'fun' of the Fair has become all-important, and has entirely obliterated the significance that once attached to the name 'Rood', it is because the institution is not looked at askance in Dumfries, as in certain ultra-'proper' communities up and down Scotland which might be named. It is altogether 'the thing' to 'do the shows' in the Queen of the South. In the course of the Fair week you may indeed see all sorts and conditions of men, with the fair sex by no means wanting, enjoying themselves to the utmost extent possible under the conditions and with the means provided.

What was it that drew such huge crowds where the 'county family does not scorn to seek amusement side by side with the town tradesman'? The principal attractions in 1907 were the shooting galleries. These came in all shapes and sizes. The traditional rifle range saw shots fired down a tunnel to sound a bell and win a prize. While, in others, suspended bottles, clay pipes or even eggshells held up by sprays of water were the targets. And 'there is the booth where cocoa-nuts stuck in cups filled with saw-dust look so easy to knock out, until you learn otherwise at the cost of some experience and not a little expenditure'.

For those who were not attracted by target practice there were novelty acts in abundance; acts that would not be acceptable in today's more politically correct world. The fat lady, married midgets, the smallest pony in the world and the sheep with eight legs were among those on offer at the Rood Fair in the early part of the twentieth century. A report in the *Gallovidian* in 1907 – entitled 'Fun of the Fair' – vividly captures the atmosphere of the event:

> Those who desire to find the Rood Fair as it really is must go down to the Sands when darkness has fallen, and the flaring naphtha lamps and dazzling electric globes have turned, by the magic of their transforming light, the double line of the dirty canvas tents and crudely painted boards into a long street of gold-glittering palaces of pleasure . . . the Rood Fair is a province of Fairyland itself!

On one memorable occasion in 1923 disaster struck the fair when a circus elephant collapsed and died on the ground at Dock Park. 'The animal weighed about three tons, and the problem of how it was to be removed baffled all the haulage experts who could be found' said one reporter. 'From noon until operations were suspended owing to darkness, a large crowd watched the proceedings, and in the end work had to be suspended.' Poor Jumbo had apparently been a feature of the fair for nearly a quarter of a century and was reckoned to be about thirty years old. The dead animal was removed the following day, but only after several failed attempts as chains snapped and even a steam engine proved unsuccessful in shifting the weighty carcass.

Of course, the attractions of the fair changed as customers became more sophisticated. Dodgems, merry-go-rounds and amusement arcades are now the order of the day but in many ways it is still true to the traditions of the past. The bright lights and noise on the Whitesands in the twenty-first century might not provoke thoughts of Fairyland but they still make for an eye-catching sight – at least for as long as the rains stay away.

3

EVERYBODY NEEDS GUID NYCHBURRIS

Jealousy can sometimes be a good thing. At least, that has been the case for the biggest single celebration on the Dumfries calendar. Guid Nychburris was, in fact, a modern invention to give the town its own 'historic' festival. Having cast envious eyes at other towns and villages across the south of Scotland it was decided that if the Queen of the South did not have its own gala day – or riding of the marches – tradition it was time to make one up.

The prime mover was Dumfries librarian George Shirley, who was a man with a mission judging by the depth of his research into the subject. His concept was to base the event on what would have taken place when the burgh received its original royal charter – believed to be in 1186. Shirley set out in the most precise manner how the ceremony would have been conducted some seven and a half centuries earlier.

While the idea of a celebration for the town seems to have been a popular one in 1932, the name of the event did not meet with universal approval, judging by letters to the newspapers. Guid Nychburris was a term taken from the Dumfries Town Council minutes of 1504. Shirley explained the selection thus:

> There is a sound historical basis for the name. We now use the word neighbour only to denote a person living next door, but in the sixteenth century it meant citizen, or fellow-townsman. Keeping good neighbourhood meant being a good citizen. . . . In

> the records of the old Burgh Court of Dumfries the word is commonly used instead of burgess. . . . Not infrequently men who had quarrelled were brought before the court and took oath to keep 'guid nychborhude' and occasionally an ally, such as Lord Maxwell, is referred to as a 'guid nychbor' to the Burgh.

This clear historical argument should have been enough to silence the critics but this was apparently not the case as the crammed postbags of the local papers of the time indicate. There was a vibrant debate in the 1930s about whether Dumfries needed this kind of festival and, if it did, what it should be called. One anonymous letter to the *Southern Scot* was scathing:

> The projected Gala will be a success, not because of the senseless title, but in spite of it. However, it is to be hoped that this anachronism is to be hung, drawn and quartered before much longer, or before it gets ineradicably rooted in the placid minds of quasi-officialdom. Why prejudice the Day with this mossy title? . . . Dumfries is not so rich in the Nychburris feeling that the Gala's birthday should be welcomed with a cold douche; it is anything but typical of this sphere of the dour Lowland Scot.

Another scribe commented:

> People are talking not about Guid Nychburris Day but about the Gala Day. Why not call it that to begin with? Excepting your correspondent most of us are plain, blunt men, who name things with a view to ease and convenience; the name above has neither, and even yet its meaning or pronunciation are a mystery to some.

Thankfully for Shirley the criticism was not universal. There were letters of support for both the idea and the name. One praised the concept in broad Scots: 'Guid Nychburris Day is rale guid, and has the merit o' bein original. . . . We dinna want a Common Ridin', they're far ower common as it is. We'll hae oor Guid Nychburris Day an' staun a'ane.'

That the man with the plan put plenty of thought into his project was beyond debate. George Shirley – librarian at the Ewart between 1903 and 1939 – was a driven man. His notes show how deeply he studied past traditions of the town to come up with the modern incarnation. The overall proposal, however, remained a simple one and has changed little in more than seventy years.

Wooden gates were to be set on the sites of the ancient town gates at Academy Street (Tounheid port), English Street (Lochmabengate port), St Michael Street (Kirkgate port) and Auld Brig port. The pursuivant and his attendants were then to be met on the outskirts of town by the cornet, his lass and lynors (supporters of the cornet). The group – by then made up of an impressive number of horses – marked out the burgh boundaries. Proceedings were then rounded off by a charter ceremony at the Midsteeple and the crowning of the Queen of the South.

That first Guid Nychburris celebration, on 22–23 July 1932, must have been something to behold. Posters promised a spectacular procession at Palmerston park depicting historical figures ranging all the way from prehistoric times to the year 1800, with representations of famous events in the history of the burgh. The four seasons were to be symbolised by 400 children. A grand concert by the King's Own Scottish Borderers was also staged at the drill hall followed by a fancy-dress dance and carnival.

Among the historical figures suggested for inclusion on that first procession were a group of Stone Age Celts, St Ninian, St Mungo, Robert the Bruce, Queen Mary, James VI, the Covenanters and, of course, Robert Burns. Notes from the programme of the first Guid Nychburris highlight the pride and importance invested in the ceremony. In many ways Dumfries was seen to be catching up with other border towns by the organisers:

> Even today, many more people know the boundaries at Hawick and Langholm, where they have been annually ridden, compared with people at Dumfries, where the practice has only been intermittent. . . . The Ridings tended to create a communal sense, a pride in the town. They made a link that drew exiled sons, who cherished memories of it from youth, back to their birthplace. They preserved affection for the home town. And gave a sense of unity to its inhabitants. Surely not undesirable things to cherish. . . . Once only in living memory have the Marches of the Royal Burgh of Dumfries been ridden – in 1901. Ancient accompaniments have been forgotten, and in projecting a revival we start with almost a clean sheet.

Shirley must have been uncertain about the festival's prospects for success but it met with almost universal acclaim. The only change made the following year was to bring the celebrations forward to June, which became their traditional date. The format for 1933 stayed the same but it was decided to use the centenary of Sir Walter Scott as the theme for the parade. 'This year a more ambitious pageant is being arranged, which will equal its predecessor in spectacular charm, but will surpass it in dramatic appeal,' promised one publicity flyer of the day. 'A dozen episodes from the rich storehouse of the Waverley Novels have been selected for presentation, and all the vivid colour and swift action of these thrilling incidents will be made to live again in The Romance of History.'

The extent to which the event grabbed the popular imagination is clearly indicated by its longevity. It has survived for decades – not without some difficulties – and remains a fond childhood memory for most Doonhamers. Watching the horses career towards the Midsteeple, gathering sweets from the floats in the parade or waiting (sometimes even in glorious sunshine) for the crowning of the Queen have become Dumfries institutions.

Only in the war years was the annual tradition broken. But it is obvious there was a hunger for its return after the horrors of that conflict. There was certainly plenty of emotion evident in the victory celebrations that were part of the event in 1946. The *Standard* rejoiced at its return:

> After being in abeyance since 1939 Dumfries Guid Nychburris festival was revived in brilliant fashion last week in conjuction with the victory celebrations. Dumfries has never been noted for its enthusiasm but on Saturday there was certainly enthusiasm on the part of the younger children who were seeing the colourful ceremonial at the Midsteeple for the first time . . . Dumfries could have had no better way of celebrating Victory Day than this revival of ancient ceremonies. It was a happy thought that peace should be symbolised in the ceremony by the Queen of the South, Miss Mary Carnochan, releasing a flock of doves at an appropriate moment.

Bonfires had burned all night on the eve of the ceremony so perhaps there were more than a few bleary eyes among the 10,000 who gathered at the Midsteeple. It was, by all accounts, a joyful day but one tinged with sad memories. None more so than when tribute was paid to three former members of the Cornets Club who had been killed in the war. Ex-cornet William Moodie and one-time Lynors Joseph Hunter and Samuel Dickie were remembered as a memorial was unveiled by the provost at Castledykes. The 1946 cornet, flight-lieutenant Kenneth Dickie, placed a wreath on a war memorial in the town after the Guid Nychburris ceremony was over. These were quiet moments in what was otherwise a day of celebration, one that gave the town a great boost in the aftermath of a long and bitter war.

By 1957 the event was so popular that it merited a huge spread in the *Weekly Scotsman*. 'Dumfries, the quiet little Border town which stands on the banks of the peaceful river Nith, is going to let her hair down in no uncertain manner,' it reported. 'It was only in 1932 that the festival was revived but since then it has gone from strength to strength and is now very much a part of the social fabric of the town. In fact, Dumfries without the Guid Nychburris festival is unthinkable.'

The year of 1961 was also an important one for the history of the event when the tradition of sending the Queen of the South along the Nith on a 'cruiser' was restarted. It proved a popular attraction but was to be dropped again in later years because of the difficulty of sending any boats along the river. Still, the 1961 celebration was rated as one of the best ever.

Queen of the South Irene Hannay was ferried down the 'royal mile' to the Greensands on a decorated barge where she got on a chestnut pony and rode to the Midsteeple. It was a memorable year also for cornet Dick Brown – who was to become such an integral part of the festivity for nearly four decades – and his lass, Kathryn Brydon. A cavalcade of around 120 was reckoned to be one of the most sizeable ever seen. This was also the year when the 'Night of the Queen's Musick' was reintroduced and proved to be a great success as over 700 people attended the drill hall. The crowd would have been bigger, but fire regulations meant that the hall could no longer accommodate the 1,600 spectators of previous years.

In many ways Guid Nychburris is taken for granted today and it now relies heavily on the commitment of a few dedicated people. Where early celebrations seemed to enjoy the support of the whole town it has become harder to get people involved as organisers. There is no town that has not seen its community spirit diluted over the years. In the era of computer games and home cinema it has been increasingly difficult for gala days to compete for the affection of locals.

The programme faced difficult times by the 1970s as reports of a financial crisis in the winter of 1974 underline. In what was dubbed 'the most crucial meeting in the history of the Guid Nychburris Entertainment Committee' members were told they had only £500 towards the £5,000 costs of the next year's proceedings. They were asked to release reserves. 'But this is like eating our seed corn,' warned the festival's vice chairman Edmund Webb, 'and until our funds are put on a more healthy basis, the future of the festival will remain in doubt.' And he issued a rallying call to the town, one which has become a familiar one in recent times. He said: 'It is up to the townspeople in all walks of life to support their annual festival. After all, Guid Nychburris Week is the only occasion in the year when the whole community has a chance to come together to demonstrate its good neighbourliness.'

It seems that this distress was at least partly addressed by 1977 when 'enthusiasm and participation' characterised proceedings. Organisers reported they were 'overwhelmed by the reaction of the Dumfries people to an event which was not long ago in jeopardy because of financial problems'. The secretary, Michael Webb, commented: 'It appears that the people of Dumfries do care for the tradition and ceremony connected with Guid Nych-burris.' The only blot on that year's landscape was the condition of some of the flags, many of which had been in use for fifteen years and were in desperate need of repair or replacement.

If locals thought their rapid response to the plight of Guid Nychburris had addressed all its problems they were sadly mistaken. But the celebrations have continued despite regular warnings over the lack of volunteers and the need to vary the attractions on offer. It is testimony to the organisers that the event was still able to go forward by the start of the new millennium.

Not even the blip caused by cancellation for the foot-and-mouth crisis in 2001 could stop Guid Nychburris for long. It would have been easy for the event to disappear altogether. However, there was a genuine desire for its return and both the organisers and the public responded well. It came back in 2002 in some style with good crowds welcoming Queen of the South Sara Brown, along with cornet Billy Geddes and his lass, Pamela Davers. Hundreds turned out and the rain that had been forecast for the day even held off. It was to be a particularly emotional ceremony for Dick Brown, now in his seventies, as he had decided to hang up his riding boots after more than forty years of service to Guid Nychburris. After missing only one event since 1959, the former cornet said farewell in style as one of around 150 horsemen and women taking part in the ride out. He was sent on his way with kind words from provost Ken Cameron: 'We all wish Dick the best for the future. Forty years is a great achievement.' It was the end of an era for both Brown and many Doonhamers as he threw his hat into the air at the Mid-steeple for one final time.

And the years ahead look reasonably bright, judging by the estimated three to four thousand who enjoyed the event in 2003. Committee member Allan Marshall rated the day a huge success and praised the main protagonists, Queen Gemma Murray, cornet Ian Nelson and his lass Kerry Walker. Changes to the programme appear to have guaranteed a good following for Guid Nychburris with the numbers taking part on the day on the up. Hopes were high of keeping increasing the number of floats in the vehicle parade in 2004 while also promoting the event more forcefully.

It may have been more than seven decades on from the audacious decision to 'invent' a historical festival for Dumfries but there are few who now doubt that it was a very worthwhile idea. George Shirley would have been delighted, and perhaps even slightly surprised, that his creation had survived into the twenty-first century. And judging by the enthusiasm surrounding the 2004 preparations for Guid Nychburris it has become a fully fledged tradition. If it was a gamble to start Guid Nychburris back in 1932 it was certainly one that has paid off.

4

INDUSTRIAL EVOLUTION

The changing tides of trade and industry will always mark the history of any town. Many factory developments or their subsequent decline are easy to explain with the benefit of hindsight. A ready supply of raw materials, a large and suitably skilled workforce, access to transport links or target markets – all of these factors play a part in the locations selected by big companies. Export costs, cheaper competition or changes in demand are the flip side that may lead to job losses and, eventually, closures.

There was surely little more natural than for Dumfries to pursue agricultural industries or textiles for its fortune. Much more astounding – at least to the modern mind – is that the town provided the base for a major car producer. Imagine Nissan, FIAT or BMW deciding to relocate to south-west Scotland; it would be unthinkable today.

Yet less than one hundred years have passed since one of the nation's top motor car producers decided that Heathhall on the outskirts of town was the ideal location to site its factory. In the early twentieth century the car was still something of a novelty but was enjoying the kind of explosion in popularity that characterised the Internet a century later. It was the flavour of the times and one of the big hitters, in Britain at least, was Arrol-Johnston.

The firm had started life in Paisley but by 1913 had made the decision to move to a new base at Heathhall. Nowadays the reasons for relocation would probably only include cheap labour, financial incentives or a reduction in overheads. Certainly proximity to the lucrative English market was a concern in the move closer to the border. Still, it appears that big business was more noble-minded in those days at least according to a collection of articles entitled the 'Industries of Dumfries and Galloway'.

> With true wisdom the directors of the firm considered the effect of the pleasant surroundings on the health of their employees, and ultimately on the quality of work they should produce. The factory was set in a beautiful place commanding wide views of a country rich in historic and literary interest. It was planned on up-to-date lines, so as to give the workers the greatest possible amount of sunlight.

Tens of thousands of cars came off the south-west Scotland production line making it one of the most important names in the early years of motorised travel. The factory was quickly switched to military use during World War I when the skills of the workforce were harnessed for other purposes. Great 500-horsepower aero engines came out of the factory to power planes that were by now essential in modern warfare. At the time around 1,500 people were employed at the plant.

If 1914–18 was a boom time then the immediate post-war years showed no sign of slowing up with 1920 a particularly impressive year for the company. It had started producing the 'dogcarts', which had been designed by founder George Johnston with the financial backing of Sir William Arrol. Later models included 12.9 and 15.9 horsepower vehicles, both of which sold extremely well and the business even branched out to Tongland, also in Dumfries and Galloway, where its Galloway cars were made. The company also produced the Empire model for overseas markets.

But competition from down south started to hit the factory as well as the general economic recession of the 1920s. It was hoped that a merger with Aster in 1927 would secure a future for the plant by bringing together the two major players in engineering. A rousing statement was issued to employees to get them to fall in behind the merger and ensure its success. In April of that year A. L. McKillop, the company secretary, issued a rallying call to employees:

> The present is an opportune time to offer a word of encouragement to our employees whose welfare is bound up with that of the company. Whilst every one is thanked for his or her past services in whatever capacity, and be it over a long or short period, it is our wish not only to secure for the greatest number a continuity of that service, but to hold out prospects of better things. A big effort is being made by the company at this time towards that end, but it must be realised that success will be achieved only in as much as each individual employee contributes his or her share of honest endeavour and help.

Initially, it looked as if the amalgamation might be just the tonic the company required. A 17.50 horsepower six-cylinder car was produced and proved very popular with customers. It was followed by a more powerful 22.4 horsepower model in 1928, which the company had great hopes for. It was certainly hailed as a great innovation at the time. One reviewer penned a glowing report on the new model:

> It is wholly free from vibration at the highest speeds, can do 55 miles an hour on third gear and 75 on top, and is said to give 20 miles per gallon of petrol and 1,800 miles per gallon of oil. We are able to show this in the coach-built saloon, but it will also be available in a fabric saloon and a coupe. The price of this new model has not been definitely been fixed, but it is anticipated that it will be about £798. . . . The finished Arrol-Aster is a well-found car, speedy and comfortable, and luxuriously appointed, a car for men

> and women of discerning taste. That it is appreciated by lovers of good motors is vouched for by their wide distribution, not only throughout Great Britain, but in the Overseas Dominions. Among other places cars from Heathhall have been recently sent out to Rhodesia, Sierra Leone, Calcutta, Nyassaland, Baghdad, Invercargill, East Africa, Ceylon, the Straits Settlements, and Australia.

As well as exporting cars the company also enjoyed success marketing Aster engines, which proved particularly popular on the high seas. Among their orders were engines for destroyers for the British, Japanese, Dutch, Danish, Swedish, American and Italian navies. The market was clearly there for Arrol-Aster products.

It was in this period that the company enjoyed one of its most high-profile successes. It helped to remodel Malcolm Campbell's Bluebird for an attempt on the land-speed record. The car reached an incredible 218 miles per hour in 1929 and although it did not break the record it did set new marks for distances of five and ten miles. It was a notable achievement for the Arrol-Aster brand.

Unfortunately, the new firm could not compete in an increasingly tough market and its days at Heathhall proved to be numbered. As orders dried up at a difficult time for businesses across the country, it was forced to close its doors in 1931. The factory itself went through a variety of different names and was mostly used for the production of rubber goods including boots and flooring (more of which later). Amazingly, Arrol-Johnston was not the only motor manufacturer in the town. For a short period at the start of the twentieth century the North British Motor Company produced more than one hundred Drummond cars from its base in the town before it too succumbed to market forces.

If the town's role as a home to the car industry was probably doomed from the start its textile and clothing industries were much more viable. Indeed, for more than a century the mills played a key part in the employment market in Dumfries – and also shaped the way the town looked. By the 1870s the mills were the dominant force in southern Scotland, and enjoyed a plentiful supply of raw material from the surrounding countryside. It is no surprise that the estimated workforce in the mills at Kingholm, St Michael Street and Troqueer – all owned by Walter Scott – totalled 1,400. The suspension bridge was constructed across the river Nith in 1874–5, primarily to allow mill workers to cross from Dumfries into Maxwelltown. By the end of the 1880s the only tweed mill not owned by the Scott family was at Rosefield mills, and it was operated by Samuel Charteris and Robert Spence.

But times got tough due to foreign tariffs and the general economic depression through the 1920s and 1930s and, after a fire in 1923, Troqueer mill did not re-open. Nevertheless, the woollen trade was still an important one for the town even in the 1960s. A guide to the town calculated that over 1,000 people were still employed in the industry with companies such as J & D McGeorge Ltd, J. A. Roberston & Sons Ltd, J. L. Gibson & Co Ltd and Wolsey Ltd. The picture is very different today and there is little left of a once-thriving sector. The Nithsdale Mills in St Michael Street were demolished and rebuilt as sheltered accommodation, the Troqueer Mills are no more while the Rosefield Mills are no longer used for their original purpose and present a sad façade to anyone walking along the Dock Park and looking across the water.

However, another piece of knitwear history survived in the town until very recently. The A. Robertson and Sons site at Saughtree, between Lockerbie Road and Annan Road, was a major player in the town for over a century. It was only early in the new millennium that it closed its doors for the final time to make way for a housing development. Many people will be unaware of its long and colourful history.

The firm was founded in the later part of the eighteenth century and its products became so well known that they appeared at the Great Exhibition of 1851 in London. The Saughtree site was purchased in 1870 and it was from there that the business operated for many decades. Apparently its wares became popular at the highest level and the company counted royalty among its customers. Through Harrods in Knightsbridge, Robertson's sold its products to King George V, and Queen Mary reputedly sent her stockings back to the firm when they required 'refooting'. Business slowed during the Second World War but was gradually built back up to pre-war levels before a takeover in the 1990s that saw the site slowly wound down until it closed in 2002 with the loss of over fifty jobs.

The Saughtree factory had barely closed its doors when local builders Robison and Davidson saw the potential to build houses on the land. And by January 2003 they had permission to build thirty-six homes – under the name of the Laurels – on what had once been an important industrial site. It was a situation mirrored by another clothing-related enterprise in the town.

The early twenty-first century saw another famous business replaced by houses. But in this case the Shortridge Laundry was only moving its base, not closing down for good. A £2.6 million housing development was planned for the College Street site, where the company had traded for more than a century.

The firm had come a long way from its humble beginnings in 1854 when Thomas Shortridge first advertised his services. In his advertisement he, 'Most respectfully begs to announce' that he had started a dyeing, cleaning and calico-glazing establishment at 1 St Michael Street, the premises formerly occupied by a Mr Beattie. Although he started off as a one-man business his techniques quickly found favour and were soon in demand. It was said that Shortridge could be spotted most mornings around six o'clock carrying water cans around his neck from the river Nith to the factory, the kind of dedication that made his business so successful. It moved to the High Street and then to Stakeford where it made its home until the start of the twenty-first century. Then it was time for a move to new premises on the Irongray industrial estate when the Stakeford site was snapped up by Loreburn Housing to build homes. A little slice of history had been transformed but at least it was not lost forever.

Such was the importance of T. Shortridge and Son during the 1920s that it was recognised as one of the 'Industries of Dumfries and Galloway' with its workforce of around 120 'women and girls'. By 1928 the appliance of modern methods had totally transformed the business as was witnessed by one visitor to the factory:

> Here again we see the application of modern scientific methods which have quite done away with the washing tub and scrubbing board, the wringer and the mangle and the hand iron which were sufficient to cope with the needs of a single household. More than that, an elaborate organisation has had to be created to ensure that each family's contribution to the vast army of shirts and collars and tablecloths and any other articles that pass through the frothy floods shall return again to the owners.

And it appears that the family business enjoyed an excellent relationship with staff, at least according to a *Dumfries and Galloway Standard* reporter who was allowed to tour the factory:

> Throughout the long history of the firm the most harmonious relations have always existed between the employers and the employed, as is evidenced by the number of employees who have spent all their working days with the firm and never wished to change. The son of Mr Shortridge's first apprentice, now a grey-haired man, still practices the art of dyeing that his father learned some eighty years ago.

It all seems a long way from the demands of modern industry and the acceptance by workers today that the job-for-life culture has disappeared forever. Still, whatever the changing circumstances, Shortridge had been a part of the Dumfries scene for nearly 160 years and has made a major contribution to the local economy.

There have, of course, been plenty of other firms that have played a large part in the working history of the town. It would be impossible to cite them all but some names will be remembered by anyone who knows Dumfries. Most of them are listed in a 1960s guide to the major local industries.

In 1964 Carnation Milk had the largest sale of any brand of evaporated, unsweetened, condensed milk in the world. And throughout the 1970s no local child's education was considered complete without a visit to the factory on the outskirts of town to see how this industrial leader made its products.

Understandably, in an area well known for dairy products, the location of the plant made good sense when it was built during the 1930s. Unfortunately, changes in market conditions had an adverse impact on the business and, although the plant came under the Nestlé banner during the 1980s, a decision was taken to close it in the late 1990s. It is now used by Dunlop's, a firm of veterinary suppliers.

Another important business that changed its name was Imperial Chemical Industries Limited, otherwise known as ICI. The business boasts Dumfries connections going back to 1939 when a group of factories were operated on behalf of the Ministry of Supply. Later, ICI's Nobel Division purchased a site on Dalbeattie Road for the production of chemical products. Among the trade names to come out of Dumfries were Cellofas, Methofas, Melinex and Propathene most of which were highly successful in the packaging industry. Even as late as 1987, ICI opened an enormous £62 million plant for the production of Melinex, which made it a world leader in polyester film and swelled the workforce to 1,200. By the late 1990s, changes in trade conditions saw ICI sell off much of its business to American giant DuPont. There was also a name change and the Dumfries facility now goes under the banner of

DuPont Teijin Films. DuPont is the world's biggest producer of polyester film, and much of it comes from Dumfries.

Finally, one business has changed its name so many times that you can guess the age of Doonhamers from the name they use for its factory. The North British Rubber Company set up shop in Dumfries in 1946, mainly to produce 'rubber footwear' – in other words, wellies – and took over the Arrol Johnston car-production site. For around twenty years it was the North British before being reinvented as the Uniroyal. About two decades on from that it became the Gates Rubber Company, a name that lasted for some time until a merger between Gates and Duralay that resulted in the creation of Interfloor. In 2005 that is still the name above the door at the Heathhall site, where the business has been operating for close to sixty years. A confusing history, perhaps, but whatever the name it is a site that has provided employment for hundreds of families.

5

THE WAR INVADERS

Dumfries was invaded twice during the Second World War. On the first occasion it was by thousands of evacuees fleeing the threatened city of Glasgow. On the second it was by Norwegian soldiers who had escaped from their own country and wanted to fight the Nazis. Both had a huge effect on the town.

The scale of the evacuation operation should not be underestimated. By September 1939 the town was bracing itself for the arrival of more than five thousand children from Glasgow – in the space of two days. During one weekend seven trains brought youngsters to their new 'homes'. The children were treated to a hot drink at Dumfries Academy before being sent out to centres in other schools and then finally being housed. It was compulsory for people with surplus accommodation to accept evacuees into their homes. If the process did not run smoothly, tribunals were promised with the possibility of children being 'redistributed'.

The county clerk for Dumfriesshire, John Robson, outlined the payments to be made to families taking evacuees: 10*s*. 6*d*. per week for one child's board and lodging; or 8*s*. 6*d*. per week for each child where more than one was taken in. Despite these payments, and the best efforts at organising the removals, it is clear from his plea to the department of health for Scotland that the town was struggling to cope. Robson said:

> It appears that mattresses and blankets are simply not available and local authorities and their officers are left to do their best in the circumstances . . . I have made inquiries as to whether mattresses and blankets can be bought but so far I have only been able to hear of the possibility of obtaining about one-twentieth of the quantity required . . . I have suggested to the authorities in Edinburgh and Glasgow that each evacuee should be asked to bring either one or two blankets with him, but I am not in a position to say yet whether that course will be followed.

Schools even considered a double-shift system to cope with the sudden arrival of new pupils. One school would use the building in the morning while the other could use it in the afternoon. As it turned out, only half the number anticipated – around 2,500 – actually arrived but it still led to ministers in the town making an appeal from their pulpits for accommodation.

There were some lighter moments. One man cycled down from Glasgow to Dumfries at four in the morning to see his wife. He arrived in the town at one o'clock in the afternoon only to have his 'spirits considerably dampened' by the news that his wife had been billeted in Moniaive. 'He thought he might be able to manage the remainder of the journey when told that Moniaive was some 16 miles distant' reported the *Dumfries and Galloway Standard*, 'but when he learned that even after he reached the upland village he would still have to travel about six miles by a not altogether satisfactory road, he felt that the task was beyond him. But the official gathered the impression that such a gallant spirit would not fail to complete his self-imposed task by some means or another.'

These were not easy times and the MP for Dumfriesshire, Sir Henry Fildes, raised his concern in Parliament about forcing unhealthy children into houses under threat of heavy penalties. When a second 'batch' arrived later the same month from Edinburgh, Rosyth, Glasgow, Clydebank and Dundee, bailie Fyfe was prompted to plead with the townspeople to be understanding: 'That misfits were inevitable is true but a little patience and give and take could solve the difficulties that arise' he said. 'Since we in Dumfries are thought to be in a fairly safe area it is at such a time not asking too much of our householders who have the available accommodation to give protection to children from areas where their safety is less sure.'

The bailie also warned against the 'objectionable feature' of people writing to the parents of evacuee children to ask them to send sufficient money to have the children removed from their homes. 'If in any case a householder thinks he has just cause to be rid of children the only way that this can be brought about is with the approval of the billeting officer and/or tribunal' warned the bailie.

If the evacuees from the big cities were misunderstood it might come as a surprise that visitors from further afield were given a warm reception. The bond formed with the Norwegian soldiers who were based in Dumfries during the war is one that lasts to this day. Out of their nation's adversity a link of great affection was formed.

Norway was one of the first nations overwhelmed by Germany and many of their young soldiers and whalers fled the country in the hope that they might regroup elsewhere. Around three hundred of them landed in Hamilton on 4 June 1940 and a few days later they were directed to Dumfries. Most of them travelled by train to the town and marched to their new quarters in the old mill building on the banks of the Nith. It must have been a spectacle indeed for the Doonhamers of the day to see the foreign 'force' striding through the streets. And their arrival was certainly a surprise since little advance notice was given to locals or, indeed, to the Norwegians.

The town clerk of the time, James Hutcheon, recounts that the chemistry was almost immediate between the Scandinavians and their hosts. By the end of their first day, he noted, they had been accepted as friends. And it a was a bond that was to strengthen in the weeks and months ahead. Hutcheon pondered the reasons for this:

> I have often wondered what was the reason for this immediate acceptance of each other. I have been told by Norwegian friends that Dumfries reminded many of them of their own towns and countryside, which was now the cause of tremendous anxiety to them in view of Nazi occupation. The Nith which runs through Dumfries is tidal. Perhaps our Norwegian friends felt that they were not as yet too far from the sea – the same sea which is ever near them in Norway.

Whatever the reasons, they settled in quickly and their numbers grew steadily. The young men were trained to be soldiers and were equipped, at first, with weapons left over from the First World War. Despite the age of their equipment they clearly made some progress as within a few weeks their reception camp was upgraded to 'Norwegian Army Camp Dumfries'. The Norway army command later moved to Dumfries and the name 'Norwegian Brigade' was adopted. By the following year the numbers topped a thousand and work got under way on building barracks at Carronbridge outside the town. In that short time they had become familiar faces around Dumfries. Hutcheon noted that they made friends wherever they went:

> It was noticed that the Norwegians, probably because they were used to knocking about in the ports of the seven seas, did not go about in crowds but spread themselves all over town, and very soon they had their own favourite little shops, wee pubs and inglenooks and places where their good-tempered, easy manners gained for them companionships which ripened into friendship.

Such was the bond between the locals and the Norwegians that a new organisation was born in Dumfries in 1941; the Scottish Norwegian Society. By the following year the first general meeting was held in Norway House – overlooking Burns Statue – with 160 members, or intending members, present. The Revd Harold Cockburn presided, with major Myrseth as vice chairman. The Duke of Buccleuch was appointed as honorary president of the branch.

Among the ideas put forward at that first meeting were to open the canteen in Norges Hus (Norway House) on Thursday evenings for meetings and other entertainment. A library was also to be set up in the building, donated by the Commercial Bank of Scotland. Among the other facilities to be offered were concerts, lectures and language classes. By 1943 the society was thriving as was highlighted by chairman Harold Cockburn's comments in the annual report:

> The society was especially proud to sponsor visits to Dumfries by the celebrated Norwegian artistes, Soffi Schonning and Waldemar Johnsen, who delighted large audiences in the Academy Hall and St George's Hall with finely varied programmes of songs, folk-songs and duets. . . . During the winter session, language classes for the benefit of Scottish members studying the Norwegian language were arranged under the direction of Lieutenant Reinholt, assisted by Lieutenant Aasen and Sergeant Borresen. Some forty members took advantage of this service. The number of Scots possessing more than a smattering of the Norwegian language is quite considerable.

In addition up to a thousand volumes were borrowed from the library over the year and the knitting circle produced gloves for the Norwegian forces!

Often there was more than friendship on the cards as the arrival of such a large number of young 'Vikings' in Dumfries did not go unnoticed by local girls. There were plenty of romances and a number of weddings throughout the war years. So much so that the local phone-book still gives plenty of evidence of the family bonds that were established.

In their turn the Norwegians were grateful for the hospitality they received. Doonhamers may be reserved by nature but they opened up their town to these strangers who shared the common bond of suffering. This mutual regard continued throughout the war as the visitors guarded sites like the airfield at Heathhall and subsequently became more active in the war.

Another effect the Norwegians had was on the sporting front. They played football at Palmerston to such a high level that they were able to take on and defeat the home side. This was little wonder; the town clerk later discovered that a number of the Norwegians had won medals in the Olympic football competition.

One occasion that typified the regard Doonhamers had for their friendly invaders was a presentation made in 1944 to major Myrseth by the Scottish-Norwegian Society at Norway House. Society chairman, the Revd Cockburn, paid tribute to the major's contribution to the town:

> They came as strangers, but it was not long before they became friends, and they had remained close friends ever since. The major, from the first, was fired with the desire to draw the Scots and the Norwegians more and more closely together. Not only had the major become a Dumfriesian by virtue of several years residence but he had dispelled all suggestion of being a mere incomer by taking unto himself a Dumfries wife. Now he was truly a native.

The major summed up the feeling of many of his countrymen who had been stationed in Scotland:

> For most of the Norwegians Dumfries had been their temporary capital city. Many in other parts of the country had said to him when going on leave: 'But we must go to Dumfries because, Major, it is our capital city.' Yes, and Dumfries would remain their capital in memory for many years, because they could never forget the friends they had found in the Queen of the South in the difficult

> beginnings of their exile. Everywhere they were met with open arms, and everything was done to give them a home from home.

With the end of hostilities in 1945 many of the Norwegian soldiers, quite naturally, returned home. But it was felt something should be done to mark the departure and a special farewell party was held, organised by the Scottish Norwegian Society. Around 250 Scots and Norwegians attended the event. And many locals did not say goodbye for ever since – thanks to a savings scheme organised by the society – a good number had gathered sufficient funds to travel over to Norway to visit their friends.

Understandably, the need for the society diminished after the war and it was eventually wound up with its funds passing on to the Glasgow branch. Nonetheless, the imprint of the Norwegian visitors is one that has stood the test of time. With the end of hostilities they did not forget their one-time home. Many stayed in the town and married local girls while the sporting link was maintained by Dumfries football side, Greystone Rovers, which even today regularly visits or hosts Norwegian outfit SK Brann.

And representatives of the Norwegian royal family have not been slow to grace the area with their presence. They recognised the fundamental role that the town played in keeping a fighting force alive for their nation. And each year on Norway's independence day there is a wreath-laying ceremony in Dumfries to remember those who gave their lives in the fight against Fascism.

The bonds were strengthened further in October 1962 when King Olav V of Norway visited the town. During his stay he stopped at Newlands – a wartime hospital for Norwegians – before travelling along Edinburgh Road and down the High Street to the Lyceum theatre past large crowds. Inside, an estimated two thousand people saw provost Watt grant the King the freedom of the town. The provost commented: 'Many memories are stirred today and we recall in particular the respect, affection and unbounded admiration which your late father, His Majesty King Haakon, was regarded by the people of this county.' And the King himself paid tribute to the debt his country still owed Dumfries.

> It was in Dumfriesshire where the first Norwegian Army came and it was here that most of them who left Norway in 1940 settled down. The friendliness and warm welcome with which they were met was a most important factor towards building up the morale and strength which made it possible for them to live through the war years separated from their families and homes in occupied Norway. Therefore, in Norway, Dumfries is a well-known name and it stands for kindness, friendliness, and hospitality.

After that it was off to Palmerston park where more school-children waved off the man who had become the youngest freeman of Dumfries. At the ground he met Queen of the South player-manager George Farm, chairman Billy Houliston and James McKinnel and his son Jimmy (the former secretary and his son, the current secretary). Then it was into a helicopter to head out of town.

And even today the link shows no sign of breaking as royal visits continue. In 2002 King Harald, Olav's son, was asked to open a new viewing area at Caerlaverock Wetlands centre. Being a keen ornithologist, and aware of the wartime friendship forged with the area, he was only too happy to say yes. It proved to be a special day for one of the few surviving 'visitors' from World War Two, Torleif Nilson, as he and wife Isabella spent more than twenty minutes chatting to the King.

While the following year there were thanks once again from the people of Norway to Dumfries as a new plaque was unveiled in St Michael's church alongside the one placed in the 1940s. A delegation led by the director general of the Norwegian ministry of defence, Elisabeth Larsen, and the consul general in Edinburgh, Grethe Knudsen, made a special visit to Dumfries to attend a church service in St Michael's and laid wreaths at the graves of Norwegian servicemen at Troqueer cemetery.

It underlined once again that despite more than sixty years having passed since the fateful day they were directed towards Dumfries neither the town, nor their Scandinavian friends, have ever forgotten the friendships forged in the dark days of war.

6

WHEN QUEENS WERE KINGS

Anyone who has spent a Saturday afternoon at Palmerston park would be hard-pressed to imagine Queen of the South at the pinnacle of Scottish football. With the best will in the world nobody strolling along Terregles Street would ever expect to turn the corner and encounter the nation's top team. Yet there was a brief moment when Queen of the South could look down on every other team in the land.

The years immediately after the Second World War produced a sporting boom with spectators eager for entertainment after six grim years of conflict. With far fewer attractions competing for attention it was unusual for football crowds to be anything other than huge and Dumfries was no exception to that general rule. Queens were probably never more popular than in the immediate post-war years and, in time, put together a team that rose higher than any side before or since.

However, things did not start well in the immediate post-war period. The position got so bad that, by season 1950/51, the Dumfries side was in the depths of the old B division. But then an amazing final rush of results – thirteen wins in the last fourteen games – saw Queens back in the top flight. The club was led by Jimmy McKinnell, who combined the posts of secretary and manager after taking over from his father in 1947 (he continued as manager until 1961 and as secretary until 1968 when the club gave him a testimonial against Celtic; he was a regular at Palmerston until his death in 1995 at the age of ninety-three).

Some of the foundations that would take them to the top of the national tree had already been laid. That promotion-winning team included goalkeeper Roy Henderson, signed from Third Lanark in 1946, New Abbey boy Dougie Sharpe in the defence and a big front man, Jim Patterson from Luncarty in Perthshire.

If Queens felt unsure in the top flight it certainly did not show and the team was bolstered for the rigours of the first division. Into the side came a midfield general in the shape of Walter 'Wattie' Rothera from Hamilton and an up-and-coming wing-half from Wishaw, Jim Greenock. Also snapped up was a full back from Arbroath, Jimmy Binning, who was to enjoy a long and successful partnership with Dougie Sharpe. The icing on the cake was the return of Jackie Oakes, who had been playing down south with Blackburn Rovers and Manchester City. Enthusiasm around the club was clearly growing in that season, 1951/52, and over 24,000 packed into Palmerston for a third round tie Scottish Cup tie against Hearts. Years later, access was granted to club minutes and it was discovered that a crowd of 26,552 had somehow crammed into the ground that day, and it is now accepted as the record attendance at Palmerston. Queens went out of the competition but their team proved more than worthy of their place in the top division.

During season 1952/53 in came promising Billy Sweeney and centre half Alex Smith from Muirkirk. But the outstanding signing was probably an outside right from East Fife, Bobby Black, who was originally from Thornhill. When Queens added Jimmy McGill to their squad a year later, from Berwick Rangers, he proved the perfect foil for Black. The team that would shock the rest of Scottish football was complete.

In truth, the momentous season of 1953/54 did not start auspiciously. After a trial game between Queens players at Palmerston – which drew a crowd of 5,000 – it was down to the group stages of the league cup, with Hibs as the visitors. Queens were turned over 4–0 and were, according to one headline of the day, 'Outplayed and Outclassed – Disappointing Start to Season'. This was followed by a narrow defeat away to St Mirren in the same competition and then a hefty 4–1 hammering at home by Falkirk. It was a depressing start to the season and 'Onlooker' in the *Dumfries and Galloway Standard* was understandably critical, as we can judge from his headline: 'Queens' Puerile Display Against Falkirk'. He went on to write:

> After Queens' plucky fight at Paisley last Wednesday, the Palmerston fans were all set for an opening victory against Falkirk on Saturday but a disappointing afternoon was in store for them. Queens have disappointed their supporters in the past, only to come away with a bang and make them forget about these disappointments. This time they certainly have something to atone for, and it was a disconsolate and critical bunch of supporters which scaled from the Terregles Street ground after Saturday's dismal showing. It would be foolish to gloss off Queens' shortcomings, and it would be difficult in any case to find an excuse for such a puerile display.

Not much mincing of words there and the team quickly tumbled out of the league cup with just a single-goal victory over St Mirren to its credit, although there was a resolute performance at Easter Road when Hibs won narrowly by two goals to one. It hardly filled supporters with confidence for the upcoming league campaign. Little could they have suspected, however, what was around the corner.

Queens came out of the traps in fine style in the league. They opened their account with a 4–1 demolition of Stirling Albion at Palmerston that put them on top of the old division one. 'Since the start of the season Queens' forwards have been dull and unimaginative, but against the Stirling eleven they threw off their lethargy and played intelligent, forceful football' noted one report. Jim Patterson opened the scoring with a penalty and doubled Queens's lead with another spot-kick. Jackie Oakes then grabbed a goal before Patterson completed his hat-trick. Albion's consolation came from Chalmers.

If Queen of the South supporters were surprised by the determination of the team at Palmerston they must have been astounded by the result achieved at Tynecastle against Hearts. The same 4–1 score line was registered as the Edinburgh outfit was easily despatched. The Dumfries boys had slipped behind as early as the sixth minute, but big Jim Patterson drew the sides level before half time. In the second half an incredible volley of three goals in three minutes at the brewery end – strikes from Rothera, Patterson and Black – broke the Edinburgh side's spirits. Queens maintained their position at the top of the table, ahead of St Mirren on goal difference. The amazement in Dumfries was summed up by the *Standard*: 'It takes quite a lot of puzzling out how the Palmerston team, which has been serving up a very mediocre brand of football since the start of the season, can unleash such power just when the odds seemed weighted against them.'

A week later and Queens were out on their own at the pinnacle of Scottish football after hammering the team level with them on points at the top of the table. St Mirren were the visitors to Dumfries and a 'disappointing' crowd of 8,500 watched in heavy rain as the Doonhamers destroyed the Paisley side. Wattie Rothera was the inspiration but once again it was a devastating burst of goals – a hat-trick in six minutes from in-form hit man Jim Patterson – that killed off the opposition after Bobby Black had given the home side an early lead.

The bandwagon moved to Firhill where the direct approach of the league leaders was too much for their struggling opponents. Patterson put Queens ahead in a first half they dominated, leaving

Partick Thistle looking ineffectual. 'Pretty-pretty interpassing around midfield took them nowhere' commented the match report. 'Direct methods brought Queens a second score.' This time it was Greenock who struck to ensure a 2–1 triumph. The following week at Palmerston it was the turn of Hibs to feel the wrath of the high-flying boys from Dumfries and Galloway. In what was dubbed 'one of the best matches in any season' Queens came out on top in a thrilling match at the beginning of October. The crowd had swollen to 16,000 as the home fans sensed this was a special season. This was a great Hibs side – the Easter Road men had won the title on two occasions in the previous three years – and they twice took the lead. But Wattie Rothera was in outstanding form. Twice he equalised for Queens and in the closing moments of a cracking game the stage was set for a dramatic winner.

> With four minutes left for play and Queens' supporters beginning to lose hope that their team would snatch the goal which their play merited, there came a dramatic finish. Rothera gained possession on the right wing and, with Hibs' defenders hesitating to go into the tackle, because they seemed to expect the cross, Rothera hit the ball with great power for goal. It entered the net via the underside of the crossbar with Patterson rushing in to make sure. It was a splendid finish to a most exciting game. Queens' supporters gave their team a great ovation as they left the field and every man in the team deserved it.

That victory put the Dumfries side four points clear at the top, with five wins out of five, and already the only undefeated team in the league. That was to change with a trip to Dens Park where Dundee demolished Queens 4–1 and catapulted themselves into second spot. It was a black day from the start with Wattie Rothera reportedly missing the train from Glasgow and only arriving by bus half an hour before kick off. Jim Patterson grabbed a consolation strike late in the game. Hardly the tonic required for the visit of Celtic to Palmerston on 17 October 1953.

But it proved to be one of the most memorable days in the history of Queen of the South football club. Any victory over the Old Firm is a rarity for a provincial side but the Glasgow giants were sitting third in the league waiting to overtake the Dumfries side. Celtic boasted many luminaries, including Bobby Evans, Bertie Peacock and John McPhail (due to injury the Parkhead side were missing one leading player, who would later become much better known in another capacity; his name was Jock Stein).

The game against Celtic – watched by a crowd of 16,000 – seemed to be following a familiar script when, after battling hard, Queens fell behind to a controversial penalty kick in the fifty-first minute. But they responded with unbelievable spirit. Rothera met a Bobby Black cross to head home an equaliser on the hour mark. And then Patterson – who else? – was in the right place at the right time once again, as the *Standard* recorded: 'Jackie Oakes came out of a tackle by Haughney with the ball at his feet and raced up the wing. Seeing Patterson running into position, he crossed hard and the ball flew off the centre's head into the net. It was a splendid goal and one worthy to win any match.' So the lead at the top of the table was back to four points. The *Sunday Mail* was suitably impressed by the Doonhamers' battling qualities, particularly those of centre half Smith who had been kicked in the head by Celtic's McPhail and 'staggered drunkenly throughout the game' but refused to leave the field for treatment. Roy Henderson also played a blinder, denying the eager Celtic forwards on many occasions.

An away draw with Airdrie preserved the Palmerston park team's position before another purple goal-scoring patch set them soaring away again. Raith Rovers – sitting in second place at the time – could hardly have expected the roasting they received on their visit to Dumfries but they were annihilated 5–1 and that was without the home side's main goal threat, Jim Patterson, who was sidelined through injury. Rovers took the lead but Rothera equalised, Black put Queens ahead and a Jimmy McGill double (his first goals for the club) put the result beyond doubt. Rothera completed the rout and in between times the Doonhamers hit the post no fewer than five times. 'The success of the Dumfries team is a source of wonder throughout Scotland' mused one scribe in the *Standard*, 'and even in their own town and district . . . supporters have been pleasantly surprised by the enthusiastic and skilful playing of the team.'

Bottom of the table Hamilton were put to the sword next with a 5–0 demolition. The scorers on a miserable wet November afternoon were the colourful combination of Black, who grabbed a double, and Brown, who struck a hat-trick. The result put Queens an incredible six points clear of Celtic at the crest of the first division.

It was not to be a kind November for the Queens, however, as defeats by Aberdeen and Clyde saw their advantage reduced significantly. But they bounced back against Falkirk at Palmerston in another high-scoring encounter. For the third time that season they netted five times but gaps in their defence were starting to appear as they conceded three. It was a match that swung on the decisions of a linesman. With the scores standing at one apiece the visitors first had a goal disallowed, which the referee had initially allowed to stand. Then Queens appealed that a shot had crossed the line and it was also given the seal of approval by the touchline official. Despite this good fortune the Dumfries side was clearly glad to get back to winning ways on the eve of one of the biggest matches of the season.

Hearts were now the chasing team in the league and the first visitors to Dumfries in December. Rothera was out injured and in stepped young George Cruickshank. Queens took the initiative and grabbed a lead in the thirty-fourth minute through Greenock, but Hearts hit back at the start of the second half through Wardhaugh. Still, Jimmy McGill had other ideas and he hit what looked like the winner just after the hour mark. But controversy surrounded Hearts equaliser from Wardhaugh in the closing stages. The supporters packed into Palmerston were convinced he was offside but there was nothing they could do about the decision to let the goal stand. The game finished two apiece and Queens had to settle for preserving a three-point advantage over their visitors.

That result may have been hard to take but there was more pleasure in store as Queens then produced another very impressive display to defeat the mighty Rangers. This was an Ibrox team with a host of Scotland stars, including Willie Waddell, Sammy Cox, George Young and Willie Woodburn. They were Rangers legends and the match was one of the most eagerly anticipated in years. Despite rain that started an hour before kick-off an impressive crowd of 18,500 rolled up to Palmerston, including several thousand away supporters who had made the journey from Glasgow. Once again it was unquenchable team spirit that won the day for Queens, as the *Sunday Mail* made clear: 'They [the spectators] had seen the Doonhamers, eager and zestful and richly endowed with team spirit . . . reduce a Rangers team to a level that had to be seen to be believed.' Queens won thanks to a double strike by Jackie Brown. It was the home side's first victory over Rangers at Palmerston and it completed a memorable Old Firm double.

Perhaps it was the incentive of a £1,000 bonus promised to the team by the chairman, Willie Boyd, if the league was won that had fired up the side. There were high hopes for the next match: 'Queens going all out to win the championship flag' trumpeted the *Standard* on the eve of the clash away to Stirling Albion after the historic win over Rangers. Unfortunately, the weight of expectation seemed to drag Queens down despite Albion's programme paying tribute to: 'One of the most popular provincial clubs in the country, their record this season is one to be proud of, and has not been gained without wonderful team spirit'. That was sadly lacking in a 3–0 defeat that allowed the chasing pack of Dundee, Hearts and Celtic to close the gap.

The Dumfries side were back on form on Boxing Day but it took them plenty of time to get into their stride against East Fife. After a goalless first half, Queens unleashed their traditional fire-power in the second period. A hat-trick from Rothera and a couple of Bobby Black strikes were enough to clinch a 5–0 win and end a memorable year. The *Standard* looked forward to 1954:

> Palmerston fans will not readily forget the year 1953 which has just ended. Away back in the early part of the year relegation worries were hovering around the Terregles Street ground . . . Palmerston has been hit by a wave on enthusiasm which has hardly been surpassed and the prospect of the league championship flag flying over the Terregles Street ground has now become more than a dream . . . Whatever the next few months may bring we will not readily forget the glory which skipper Alex Smith and his men have achieved.

Sadly, it was a dream that died at the start of 1954. On a 'Black Ne'erday for Queens' the Dumfries side lost on 1 January to St Mirren away and were then dumped 6–2 by Partick Thistle at Palmerston the following day. Maybe the toll of being a small club challenging the big boys was starting to tell. The league leadership went to Hearts and the season drifted away.

The team managed just five more wins that season and never led the table again. Indeed the club slid down the division to finish the campaign in tenth spot. Still, it was a memorable year in the history of Queen of the South. For a short while at least the Doonhamers looked down on the big names of Scottish football, and a trip to the south-west was one that no side relished. It is a position to which the Doonhamers have never returned but the memories of that team still echo around Palmerston park. As long as people continue to talk about the amazing events of the 1953/54 season there is still the hope that maybe, just maybe, Queen of the South might rule the Scottish football scene once again just as they did for half a season fifty years ago. It is the kind of dream that keeps fans paying for their place in the ground come Saturday afternoon, no matter how many doses of reality they might have imbibed over the years.

7

BASHER, THE CLOWN PRINCE AND THE TIN MAN

Most football fans know that their average Saturday afternoon is dominated by the dull and monopolised by the mediocre. Thrilling matches are the exception rather than the rule and moments of sublime skill are usually in short supply. That is what makes the great players and entertainers so precious. One touch, move or breathtaking save may be all there is to cherish from a cold, damp Scottish league fixture. The footballers who can raise the game above the mundane – if only for a moment – are a special breed.

Queen of the South have had a few of those special players since the club's formation in 1919. Those early years saw Hughie Gallacher strut his stuff before he was quickly snapped up by Newcastle United and became a legend on Tyneside. And there have been so many other greats at Palmerston: Wattie Rothera, Jim Patterson, Jackie Oakes, Bobby Black, Allan Ball, Peter Dickson, Tommy Bryce, Andy Thomson, Peter Weatherson and Steve Bowey among them.

In many ways it is unfair to single out players for special attention when football is a team sport but there are a few who stand out. Not many, after all, can claim to have gone to Wembley and helped hammer the English while plying their trade at Palmerston. Yet that is exactly what Billy 'Basher' Houliston – a bustling centre forward – did in 1949.

A Doonhamer born and bred, Houliston played with local schools Brownhall primary and Dumfries High before signing for Queens in October 1945. In 1949 he got his first cap for Scotland at the age of twenty-eight and struck the winning goal in a dramatic 3–2 victory over Northern Ireland at Hampden in the home international championships. Both player and ball ended up in the back of the net on that occasion underlining the wholehearted approach to the game that the Palmerston hero had. But his finest hour was just round the corner.

For the climax of that season's home internationals Scotland were due to go to Wembley to take on an England side that regarded itself as one of the best in the world. Even north of the border there were reservations about the inclusion of the raw Queen of the South recruit but, despite that fact, 30,000 Scotland fans made the traditional trip to Wembley for the clash with the Auld Enemy in April 1949. They were not to be disappointed and Houliston played a starring role.

'Scotland's Victory at Wembley – Houliston's Leadership' trumpeted the *Standard* with justifiable pride. To this day he remains the only player to don the dark blue of the full international side while at Palmerston. Little wonder there was such immense satisfaction at seeing him lead the line so powerfully in a win over England at Wembley. The *Standard's* report on the game went on:

> Billy Houliston, the Queen of the South centre forward, the first footballer from the South of Scotland to play for Scotland against England, although not a goal scorer played a prominent part in England's defeat at Wembley. There had been a good deal of criticism about Houliston's selection, as indeed there had been about the whole Scottish team, but the eleven completely justified themselves and their sponsors by returning a victory when the critics were practically unanimous in predicting a defeat.

The Scots took the lead after twenty-nine minutes through Mason and never looked back. Houliston played a big part in setting up the second goal for Steel at the start of the second half and Reilly completed the rout soon after. This was no second-string England side that Scotland put to the sword as legendary figures such as Stanley Matthews, Tom Finney, Billy Wright and Stan Mortensen were part of the team along with their sole goalscorer on the day, Jackie Milburn, known affectionately as 'Wor Jackie'. The papers noted that England neither took kindly to defeat nor to the tactics adopted by our Billy. The *Standard* reported: 'Houliston, up against a powerful centre half in Franklin, had to use all his weight and strength and it was not relished by the English defence.'

The *Daily Record* paid tribute to the Queens man's display thus: 'The English defence became unsettled with one eye on the ball, the other on Houliston who was springing up unexpectedly all over the Saxon defensive area . . . [English officials] were sharply critical of Houliston who, they thought, was a bit on the robust side, but Billy needn't worry his head about that. The Dumfries man adopted the right tactics.'

The team was dubbed the Wembley Warriors for a robust approach that put the opposition off its stride. It was Alex James – one of the Wembley Wizards of 1928 – who picked out Houliston for his display and recalled another former Palmerston great. He commented: 'Maybe Houliston isn't another Hughie Gallacher, but he rumbled the English defence, and boy, how he got stuck into them!' While the *Daily Mail* also recognised the importance of his efforts. It opined: 'Every player achieved success in the part he had set out to play and if Houliston appeared over-robust at times, it must be remembered that football is a man's game. His manliness had the desired unsettling effect on the defence.'

Apparently Houliston was booed by the English fans for his tough approach but he would not have cared. At the end of ninety minutes Scotland had not only secured a major victory but also clinched the home international series for 1949. The ends, as the saying goes, justify the means. It was Houliston's finest hour and, although he only won three caps – all in 1949 – Scotland won all three matches. It was also a proud moment for Dumfries to have a local boy and Queen of the South player silence Scotland's greatest rivals.

The reaction in Scotland to the win was ecstatic. As the *Royal Scot* pulled into Glasgow's Central Station on the Sunday with the team on board there was near hysteria, as the *Daily Record* observed: 'Massed 10,000 strong, sweeping through crush barriers, thrusting police and railwaymen aside, an army of hero-worshipping fans stormed Glasgow Central Station last night to greet Scotland's Wembley Warriors.'

While there was plenty of success with Scotland it was on international duty that Houliston's playing career was cut short. On a tour of America in the summer of 1949 he picked up a serious ankle injury, which left him to make the long journey home on the *Queen Mary* without the rest of the squad. Although he left the Queens in 1952 for Berwick, and then Third Lanark, he was never quite the same player again and hung up his boots in 1953. Houliston remained a prominent figure in Dumfries through his work as a publican, and as a director of Queens, before retiring from the board in 1994. He died in 1999 at the age of seventy-seven but the memory of the Doonhamer who tamed the English will live long in the memory.

Houliston was the only Queens player to be capped by his country. But few supporters have any doubt about who was the finest from their side never recognised by Scotland. Houliston's teammate, Roy Henderson – once dubbed the 'Clown Prince of Keepers' – was a hero at Palmerston but always found the path to the Scotland shirt blocked, usually by Bobby Brown of Rangers or Jimmy Cowan of Morton. Nevertheless he was held in such high regard by the Palmerston faithful that they even voted him their favourite player of all time nearly fifty years after he hung up his gloves.

Henderson was born in Wishaw but signed for Queens from Third Lanark in 1946. He was far from the tallest of keepers – being under six feet tall – but those who saw him play reckon he made up for this by outstanding positional sense and agility. Although his debut for the Doonhamers was one he would want to forget – a 9–1 drubbing by Hibs at Easter Road – there were many fine moments in almost four hundred appearances for the club.

He helped the team win the second division championship in 1951 and was also a part of the famous Queens team that topped the old first division table at Christmas 1953. But his most memorable game, for a variety of reasons, was a Scottish Cup semi-final against Rangers in April 1950 at Hampden Park. It was the first time Queens had come so close to the final and the anticipation in the town was immense. It was a real mismatch in league terms: Rangers were breathing down the neck of Hibs at the top of the first division while Queens were sitting second bottom of the A Division with only Stirling Albion below them. Only a miracle was going to stop Queens from being relegated but there was still the glamour of the cup. Most of those in the know agreed with the following newspaper preview of the semi-final: 'There are many who feel that Queens chances of appearing in the final are slender, and when we consider the cup record of Rangers, such a view is not surprising.' But the game would be a special one for Henderson in particular, since it pitted him against the team he had idolised as a boy.

Some 53,000 fans were at Hampden for a game that Queens started strongly. A goal from Jackie Brown gave the Doonhamers the lead and then Henderson performed heroics to keep his favourite side at bay. But when the Rangers equaliser came it was something of a calamity and must have been a real heartbreaker for the flamboyant net-minder and the rest of his team. A report in the *Dumfries and Galloway Standard* captured the moment:

> A dangerous flag-kick by Waddell was picked out of the air by Henderson and no one was worried when, in fourteen minutes, Rangers were awarded yet another corner kick at the other end. Rutherford's kick was among the poorest he'll ever take, yet as valuable as any he'll ever place to perfection, for from it came the equaliser. Scarcely head high, the ball came straight towards Sharpe, standing right out of the goal and a few yards out. With the back all set to clear, Henderson shouted 'Right Dougie', Dougie ducked and out came the keeper to gather the ball in upturned arms. The vice didn't close properly, the ball squirmed over Henderson's shoulder, touched George James, and trickled over the goal-line.

It does not take much to imagine the agony that must have followed this disastrous equaliser. Try as they might the Doonhamers could not bounce back and the match ended 1–1. The replay was a one-sided affair – with the Dumfries boys perhaps having given their all in the first match – and the Glasgow giants triumphed 3–0.

It would be unfair, however, to remember Henderson for conceding that goal in the semi-final. His overall performances were excellent and he came close to the full Scotland honours that his talents undoubtedly merited. He was called up on no fewer than six occasions as reserve keeper for his country but never made that final step into the full national team.

Nonetheless, he was rightly held in the highest regard at Palmerston park. His bravery in goal could never be called into question and it was this raw courage that cost him his worst moment between the sticks. It happened in 1956 away to Dunfermline. A clash with Pars centre-forward Charlie Dickson saw him break his leg at the start of the season and he was ruled out for most of the campaign. Although he did try to make a comeback, he was never quite the force he was before the injury and decided to retire at the end of season 1956/57.

Henderson died in Dumfries in 1997 but seven years after his death his memory lived on. The *Dumfries and Galloway Standard* ran a poll to find out who supporters rated as their 'Greatest Ever Doonhamer'. The result was a landslide victory for Henderson, seeing off many illustrious colleagues who went on to play for bigger teams or who were capped by their country. Perhaps the fact that their favourite son was never recognised by Scotland made the people of Dumfries keen to recognise his achievements.

The great goalkeeper was one of the most entertaining players ever to grace Palmerston but his mantle as 'Clown Prince' was taken on by a young dribbler who came on the scene in the 1980s. Ted McMinn, nicknamed the 'Tin Man', was only with the Doonhamers for a short time but he enjoyed an incredible career and was certainly unique in a game that was rapidly becoming a big-money business.

Born in nearby Castle Douglas in 1963, McMinn's early career at St Ninians primary and Maxwelltown High School was not a glittering one. As a teenager with Dumfries High former pupils' team he hardly set the heather alight for his manager. 'He broke me in gently and never gave me a game for two years – and I only got that by accident' quipped Ted, whose real name was actually Kevin. It was only when the squad was down to ten men that he was picked to play.

The gifted dribbler went to junior club Glenafton but it was not long after that his hometown team moved in for him. The transfer fee was the stuff of legend with £325 and 1,000 lottery tickets securing his services in 1982. He was working at Robertson's Sawmill when Willie and Sammy Harkness of Queen of the South made their bid. 'Before they even said anything I knew I wanted to sign for them' he once commented. 'Even if I'd had to give them money I would have signed.'

It was the start of a short, sparkling spell of sixty-seven games that lit up Palmerston park. Part of McMinn's attraction was his ungainly running style, which made it hard for the opposition to work out what he was going to do next. It was often thought that even the man himself was not entirely sure of what he wanted to do with the ball. Nonetheless he mesmerised defenders and eventually secured a £100,000 transfer to Rangers under manager Jock Wallace – a record transfer fee for Queens at the time. According to the official club history, Ted had been scouted several times by English giants Newcastle United but surprisingly the Tynesiders did not make a bid for his services.

McMinn won the hearts of Rangers fans with one particularly impressive performance against Celtic. And he was chosen to feature on a video of 'great entertainers' that highlighted the most gifted players to play for the Ibrox club. It is perhaps no accident that he was remembered by former team-mate Terry Butcher as the only man who could dribble six players, fall over the ball and still get a standing ovation from the home support.

McMinn found that he did not fit in under the new Souness regime at Ibrox and he was transferred to Seville – now managed by his old gaffer, Jock Wallace – for a fee of £200,000. When Wallace left he became unsettled and returned to Derby County in a £300,000 deal. It was in this period that he played the best football of his career having been made club captain at the Baseball Ground. He was touted for inclusion in the Scotland world cup squad at Italia '90 and might have made it but for ligament damage that ruled him out of the game for fourteen months.

His career took him from Derby to Birmingham and then to Burnley as he mixed right moves with wrong ones, just as he did on the field of play. After retirement he stepped into management, often teaming up with old friend Mark Wright. By 2004 he was back in the management game, even if it was at a relatively low level as assistant manager at Mickleover Sports Club in the Northern Counties East football league. 'As a player I hated losing and it's no different in the position I'm now in' he told the local paper shortly after signing up. 'I was itching to get back into football and I love being involved in the game.' Same old Ted McMinn, obviously, with the infectious enthusiasm that made him so popular at Palmerston in his all-too-short reign. But he rightly deserves recognition as one of the most entertaining players ever seen at the Dumfries ground.

8

GHOST TOWN

Any town that has been around for at least eight centuries will have more than its share of eerie tales. Throw in a little bit of historic bloodshed, tales of long-lost love and a few impudent spirits and you have all the necessary elements for some spooky goings-on. Add to that a series of dark closes and underground passages criss-crossing the place and things really hot up.

Dumfries can certainly lay claim to more than its share of ghostly stories and sightings. The town centre on a foggy winter night still makes most pedestrians a little uneasy. There is certainly evidence – both anecdotal and a little more concrete – that spectres like to stride the streets that seem so safe and unassuming during the day. And although we like to think that we have much more cynical and sophisticated minds when it comes to explaining the supernatural there has been no let-up in the number of inexplicable occurrences. Indeed, even the twenty-first century has thrown up a number of mysteries.

That there should be plenty of tales from years gone by is hardly surprising. These were times when stories of ghosts and ghouls were the order of the day and many were gripped by the belief that visitors from beyond the grave were nothing out of the ordinary. One of the most famous tales of the nineteenth century was that of the Troqueer ghost – recounted by the *Gallovidian* magazine in 1907 – and it ably illustrates how readily people accepted spooky explanations for something that was, in reality, much more down to earth. It dates from 1826 when rumours were rife of a ghostly presence in the area. One man even testified to spotting a white figure coming from the Kirkyard, but said that the apparition's footsteps were inaudible. 'This story, with the eerie additions of the noiseless footfall spread far and near and infected with fear all and sundry as might the presence of a plague, and no-one ventured out-of-doors after dark unless under dire necessity' it was reported.

But one brave soul, Deacon Gillies, had his suspicions not only about the ghostly figure but also about the recent disappearance of a number of bodies from the Troqueer churchyard. He waited until a boy was buried in the graveyard and then lay in wait for the 'ghost'. He was not disappointed as a 'figure all white and rigid' appeared shortly after nightfall. But its next action was 'rather unghostly' as it whistled for an accomplice to come and join it. The two figures headed toward the fresh grave and the deacon, who could control himself no more, fired a warning shot. The story ends the following morning when one of the 'ghosts' – actually a would-be body snatcher shot by Gillies – was found lying dead across the partly opened grave. So, the mystery had been solved and the cash earned by providing bodies for dissection in Edinburgh was the real reason for these spectral appearances.

Another strange graveyard tale is linked with St Michael's church where, of course, Rabbie Burns found his resting place. But it is not the grave of the Bard that gives rise to this superstition but a rather less-exalted name. A pillar marks the epitaph of William McCracken of Lochvale, a writer from Dumfries. According to local legend, retold in the *Gallovidian* by Thomas Dykes, some strange sounds could be heard emanating from 'beyond the grave':

> Behind the base are three cup-like hollows which have been worn away by little clogs and boots. The boys of many generations believed and still practice the art of 'black magic' in performing a rite. One boy places a handkerchief – preferably of silk – over the

> oval recess and listens, while his accomplice proceeds round the back and vigorously kicks the base. If he kicks hard enough, the listener is supposed to hear 'His Satanic Majesty' growling and rattling his chains and roaring imprecations.

Strange stuff indeed, although the writer confesses that despite various attempts to provoke a reaction during his childhood there was never any response. A bizarre superstition perhaps, but one that clearly exercised a grip on local youngsters until quite recently. It is intriguing to imagine just how the rumour started – and what allowed it to last for so long.

Much more straightforward to understand, if not explain, is the tale of the ghost of Bonnie Prince Charlie, which was alleged to haunt the old County hotel – where the Next clothes shop used to be and which, in 2005, is the site of Ottakar's bookshop on Dumfries High Street. It is a historical fact, of course, that the Prince stopped off in Dumfries in 1745 and made his infamous demand for £2,000 and 1,000 pairs of shoes for his army from the people of the town. He also set up headquarters in Dumfries until he was forced to flee north due to lack of support for the Stewart cause.

What makes this ghoulish tale so intriguing is that the most famous sighting was by a person largely unaware of the history of the site. Staying in the County hotel in 1936 a guest in the upper lounge reported seeing a man, dressed in Jacobite garb, appear from a doorway. The man stopped – apparently deep in thought and looking more than a little troubled – before turning away and going back through the same door. It later transpired that the door had heavy furniture blocking it and there was no way anyone could have got through; at least, no normal human being.

The upper lounge, the guest later discovered, was known as Bonnie Prince Charlie's room. When the Prince stopped in Dumfries almost two centuries earlier, he had slept in the room on the other side of the disused door. Much of the room had been retained in the style pertaining at the time of Charlie's visit, including the panelling. The décor, which included a Royal Stewart tartan carpet, also paid tribute to the famous guest. None of this information was known to the twentieth-century guest who spied this worried Jacobite figure, which many believe to have been the ghost of the Prince.

It is interesting that the tale has survived, despite the fact that the ghost has not been spotted for the best part of seventy years. When Ottakar's moved into the building during 2003 the company was well aware of the history of the site: 'We'll show him a fine welcome if he visits again,' the store manager told the *Standard*. 'But he'll not get any shoes out of us!'

Many ghostly apparitions are famous figures who have reputedly lived in an area or passed through at one time or another. It should come as no surprise that Robert the Bruce and Roger Kirkpatrick – who together killed the Red Comyn at Greyfriars in 1306 – have also been the subject of a number of alleged sightings. The best known came from some Norwegian servicemen. The visitors clearly had strong imaginations, or perhaps were more open minded, since they are at the heart of a couple of local spooky tales.

The sighting of the famous historical killers was made in Dumfries town centre in 1944. Two Norwegians were walking down Castle Street late one night when they spotted a pair of figures running away from them. Their reports claimed that the duo looked as if they had carried out a terrible act and were fleeing the scene of the crime. As they sped off towards the river Nith the two foreign servicemen were not entirely sure what they had witnessed.

Obviously they were unlikely to be aware of the history of the area, which makes their sighting all the more interesting. It was reputedly not until after the event that the two witnesses realised that, despite the fact that they had seen the two men running away on a cold night, they had not heard any footsteps. Their silent flight made what the pair had seen all the more suspicious – and more difficult to explain. Of course, they were standing almost exactly where the notorious killing took place more than six hundred years earlier. This was where Robert the Bruce sent Kirkpatrick to 'mak siccar' that Red Comyn was dead. Could these two strangers really have seen Bruce and his faithful retainer?

It is also said that a spectre with a less famous name was spotted by Norwegians in Second World War Dumfries. This occurred in almost exactly the same place as the Bruce sighting and it too is extraordinary. If ghosts are often linked to great historical events, they are perhaps even more frequently attached to desperate love stories. That was the case in the ghost of 'MacMilligan', or 'McGilligan', which reputedly appeared in 1940.

Once again it was the area between Castle Street and the Nith that gave rise to the apparition. A Norwegian stationed in Dumfries was returning to his billet late on a summer evening when he saw a terrible sight: the headless horseman, a classic figure in many ghost stories.

According to the young serviceman's report, the figure had charged across the road just a few yards in front of him before eventually dissolving into the one of the buildings. All of which must have left the poor Norwegian shaken and desperately seeking an explanation for what his eyes had just witnessed. The answer, from a supernatural point of view, was that this was not the first manifestation of the ghost of MacMilligan.

The story goes that the unfortunate horseman had been courting a local girl several centuries earlier and had gone to visit her. However, her brothers had not taken kindly to his attentions and warned the young suitor off. He fled in fear and charged off on his horse. But he was to meet a very unfortunate end. In the darkness he had not spotted a low, overhanging branch, which took his head clean off. The head rolled and ended up at the gates of Dumfries priory, close to the site where the Norwegian met the ghost.

It was not the first time the headless horseman had been seen.

From time to time stories had surfaced of the ghost being seen in and around the same places. The spirit was reputed to be in search of the head lost so long ago. And that is what had crossed the young Norwegian's path in 1940.

An equally spooky tale concerns the Lincluden piper, which is told in Armstrong's *Visitor's Illustrated Guide to Dumfries and Vicinity* (1894). The tale centres on the subterranean paths that criss-crossed old Dumfries, in particular a path that linked the castle of Dumfries to the abbey of Lincluden. It was here that a poor piper is reputed to have met his end. The tale is one not uncommon in other parts of Scotland and may well derive from the sometimes ghoulish skirl of the pipes.

The story is that a group was seated in the Grey Horse in the Vennel when an old blind piper made the claim that there was an underground passage running to Lincluden abbey. The 'jovial core' challenged the old man to prove his argument by making the journey he claimed was possible as Armstrong's *Guide* records: 'The conversation was running on an assertion made by the piper that the passage really existed, when he was challenged to thread it from the Auld College end, the entrance being from the basement of the refectory.'

The blind piper accepted the challenge and at the 'mirk o midnight' went deep into the passageway playing his pipes. But instead of re-emerging – either from the same end or somewhere further along – he was never seen again and disappeared into the underground tunnel forever. The spooky story ends with a claim that the pipes could be heard playing from the passageway every night at the hour the old piper entered the tunnel.

A better-known ghostly figure in Dumfries folklore is that of the Grey Lady, a young Victorian woman reputed to haunt the Kings Arms hotel. The story was given a little modern authentication in 1996 not long after Boots opened its store near the site. This is another tale of a broken heart since the Grey Lady is thought to be the ghost of Jane – daughter of provost Robert Jackson – who died of a broken heart when her love, captain Robert Stewart, was killed in the French revolutionary wars.

Jane's ghost was 'seen' by patrons in the King's Arms hotel, but the modern version spooked six Boots sales assistants. They were taking part in an evening training session when one reported: 'First we heard a squeaking noise like the wheels of a trolley. After a short pause there was a bang. Then we heard the buttons on the digital lock on the door being pressed and the door opened. It was one of the most frightening things I've ever encountered.' Further investigation found nothing, but it was enough to ensure that the legend of the Grey Lady is one that lasts to this day.

Also fresh in the mind are stories of a supernatural presence at the Globe Inn in the town centre. Many mysterious goings-on there have been attributed to a mischievous spirit. One of the most recent came in 2002 when a bunch of keys that had been missing for six months strangely reappeared. The incident occurred while a film crew was working on a project about Rabbie Burns, who famously drank in the pub. The keys were to an upstairs room and had been hunted for high and low – only to be spotted on the floor of the hall beside the door. The only explanation that staff could offer was that they had been returned by the ghost who had enjoyed a joke or two at their expense over the years.

Manageress Jane Brown told the *Standard*:

> I always lock the upstairs room, the Howff Club room, and I leave the keys hanging in the door but about six months ago they went missing and we searched everywhere. . . . Then one of the girls with the film crew found them at the door, exactly where they would have been if they had fallen out of the lock and the exact place I looked when they first went missing. The ghost has been quiet recently but in the past there have been a number of times that mischievous things have happened. Our piper Callum

> Watson once had his pipes knocked over while he was playing. Doors sometimes slam shut, lights are switched off and one time I was in a locked room when all fourteen curtains went up then back down again. But I believe the ghost isn't harmful, only mischievous, and I am happy living with it.

And so the ghostly goings-on in Dumfries show no sign of letting up in the twenty-first century. Be they famous historical figures, characters from tragic love stories or just spirits with a sense of fun there is plenty of material in the town for those who believe in the spirit world. And for as long as the tales are told and there are enough fertile imaginations around – or people with minds open to visitors from the 'other side' – there are sure to be more sightings in the years to come.

9

DEADLY DOONHAMERS

There is a dark side to Dumfries that it is easy to forget. But a look around at the monuments and buildings that mark the town bring back just how prominently death and infamous killings have featured in its history. Any walk through the heart of the Queen of the South is likely to take you past a site with a deadly link.

Of course, the old Greyfriars site, across the road from where the church stands today, was where the Red Comyn met his end at the hands of Robert the Bruce and Kirkpatrick. While the Whitesands proudly boast a memorial to James Kirko, a Covenanter killed by English dragoons in the seventeenth century. Not far away from that is reckoned to be the spot where nine alleged witches were burned at the stake in 1659. And Buccleuch Street housed the old prison where the gallows stood for regular public executions.

Even our claim to the legacy of Robert Burns has its morbid side. After all, Dumfries is the place where he died, not the place where he was born. Famously it was the waters of the Brow Well, near Ruthwell, which he took to in an attempt to reverse a serious illness. Unfortunately, it seems they might have had the opposite effect since he passed away not long after trying to make use of their 'healing' powers in 1796.

One of our darkest claims to fame, however, was the town's long-lasting love for public executions. It is believed that the last people to be hung in front of a crowd in Scotland met their fate in Dumfries. Large crowds were in attendance on both occasions.

In 1862 Mary Reid, or Timney, was charged with the murder of her neighbour Ann Hannah at Carsphad, in the parish of Kells. Despite many efforts to have the death sentence commuted she was sentenced to death. It is not difficult to imagine the distress in Dumfries prison on the Monday before the execution when she was visited by her husband and two children. She had to be dragged away from her children as they were shepherded out. A crowd running into many thousands turned out on the morning of 29 April 1862 for the grisly event.

It was a case that attracted much attention given the apparent mental frailty of the accused and Lord Deas, the presiding judge at the circuit, is said to have been jeered in the streets of Dumfries after the trial ended. There was no doubt, according to reports of the time, that Timney had beaten her victim to death with a wooden 'beetle' but she was described as 'a poor, ignorant, feeble-minded Irishwoman of excitable temperament'. Because of that, and the belief that there was a relationship between her husband and the murdered woman, there was some sympathy for Mary Timney. This, and the relative rarity of the occasion – the last public execution prior to this had been that of James McManus who was hanged in 1826 for robbing a farmer on his way back from Lockerbie lamb fair – may explain the numbers that turned out to watch her gruesome end. As one reporter wrote:

> Thousands of townspeople gathered early on the morning round the prison, and their numbers were augmented by many from the surrounding country, some of whom had travelled long distances in order to witness the sorrowful spectacle. The convict was brought onto the scaffold by a high window in the gable of the prison facing towards Castle Street, and when confronted with the instrument of death and the terrible sea of faces she uttered a shriek and cast around her a wild look that long haunted those who saw it.

This particularly macabre piece of Dumfries history had another twist more than thirty years after the event. In 1893 the Clydesdale Bank Company purchased a slice of old prison land and were carrying out excavation work over the area that used to be the exercise yard on the female side of the jail. While excavating the foundations for the new bank building, workmen made a grim discovery. When cutting a trench at a depth of about five feet they came across a coffin embedded in the wet clay. It turned out to be the final resting place of Mary Timney, who had been buried in the prison grounds. Nowadays the area would have been swiftly cordoned off but it appears that, at the end of the nineteenth century, there were no such sensitivities as many people gathered to see what was going on before action was taken.

As a report of the day said:

> Intelligence of the discovery spread quickly through the town, and in a short time a crowd of several hundred people had collected in Buccleuch Street and St David Street anxious to secure a glimpse of the gruesome relics. Several constables were placed on duty to keep them outside the hoarding which encloses the site, and then the remains were screened from view.

The body was later removed from the site and the crowd quickly left the scene. Some time thereafter Timney was re-interred in St Michael's cemetery having been disturbed in her previous resting place.

If there was a degree of sympathy with Mary Timney this was certainly not the case for the last man executed in the town, which was also the last public hanging in Scotland. Robert Smith was convicted of raping and strangling an 11-year-old girl in Croftshead wood between Cummertrees and Annan. He stole nine shillings and eleven pence from her. In a desperate attempt to cover up his crime he tried to shoot a woman who could place him with the girl but was scared off before he could fire. The evidence against Smith was conclusive and he was sentenced to death on 12 May 1868.

The 19-year-old went to his death in front of a crowd estimated at six hundred. Judging by accounts of the proceedings the appetite for public executions appeared to have diminished despite the heinous nature of the crime. A number of the crowd were reported to have run away when the rope was put round Smith's neck on the gallows outside the prison wall. To make matters worse, the rope had not been fitted correctly and it took the young man about fifteen minutes to die. As soon as he was pronounced dead he was lowered from the noose and a plaster cast was taken of his head. That cast was kept for viewing in Dumfries museum.

These dreadful scenes went out of fashion as executions were first removed from the public eye and then made illegal by statute. But murder held a morbid fascination for Doonhamers, as witnessed some sixty years later with the coverage of the 'Coffee Close Tragedy'. In this case, Arthur Pepper was accused of killing Annie Mather at her home in Coffee Close. Pepper was a driver with a travelling show and for ten years had been in the habit of living with Mather whenever he was in Dumfries.

The story hit the headlines when the woman's body was discovered:

> A tragedy of a character fortunately rare in Dumfries took place within a house in the Coffee Close, Queensberry Street, on Monday morning, when Annie Mather, 35 years of age, a native of Thornhill district, was found dead with her throat cut. . . . The tragic discovery was made shortly before ten o'clock and caused a painful sensation in the town.

The house was situated in a tenement over a confectionery shop in Queensberry Street. Only a few moments earlier the young woman had been seen at the child welfare centre in Buccleuch Street getting milk for her two children. She stopped to chat to people on her way home before going back inside. Two neighbours heard her screaming for help and rushed to the flat where they saw Mather lying on the ground; she was covered in blood and 'kicking about but unable to speak' said one witness. A voice from behind the door ordered them to get out, and this they did but the police were called and a razor was found in the room. Shortly after, Pepper was arrested and charged with murder.

Not only was there heavy coverage in the newspapers of the time but also a great deal of public interest and this resulted in a packed court when the trial started on 27 April 1926. The police surgeon for Dumfries – Dr Joseph Hunter – testified that Pepper 'was the least murderous man he had ever come across'. In addition an expert in 'lunacy' was called by the defence to explain the actions of Pepper on the morning he was alleged to have killed Mather. His conclusion was that there was no current evidence of insanity but there may have been on the morning of 8 February when the unfortunate woman died. As one report of the proceedings noted:

> He came to the conclusion that on that morning at the time the murder occurred the accused was in what was called a state of fugue, a trance-like state, or in a state of automatism. When in that condition a person was not conscious of what he was doing. . . . His whole nature had changed, and immediately after he changed into a violent state he resumed his previous stolid and indifferent state.

The judge went to great lengths to explain to the jury exactly what they had to decide upon in reaching a verdict. He was keen to highlight what he felt was at the heart of the case:

> The crux of the case . . . was whether or not the man was mad in the sense the speaker had stated, in the sense of being an irresponsible

> creature, a madman, whether or not on that particular day and that particular hour he was, or was not, suffering from some kind of mental aberration which had the effect of freeing him from any responsibility.

Members of the jury were clearly convinced that Pepper was in some kind of trance at the time as it took them only thirty-seven minutes to come to a conclusion. By twelve votes to three a guilty verdict on the lesser charge of culpable homicide was brought in and the accused was sentenced to seven years in prison.

But what were the reasons for Pepper's uncharacteristic actions? He was said by neighbours to be a quiet man and very kind to Mather; not at all the sort of person who would be violent to a woman. It seems that his motivation was jealousy. Annie Mather had taken in a lodger – Samuel Murdoch – and Pepper may have been afraid that he was going to be replaced in his partner's affections. The trial judge, Lord Alness, clearly thought so and even quoted lines from Shakespeare's play *Othello* in his summing up to illustrate that people do kill their loved ones out of jealousy.

If this killing caused a stir locally there was a national media focus on Dumfries twenty-five years after the Pepper case. A shooting in a quiet south-west town would have been shocking enough, but when the victim was an on-duty police officer the impact was even greater. Sergeant William Gibson, constable Andrew Hope and constable Robert Campbell were called out at around three o'clock on a May morning in 1951 following reports that a 'madman' was on the rampage and threatening anyone who crossed his path. Gibson was driving, with Hope at his side, and Campbell was in the back of the car. They came across 30-year-old Robert Dobie Smith – of 20 Holm Avenue, Dumfries – as they turned off High Street into Bank Street. Sergeant Gibson stopped the car and said to Smith: 'What are you doing lad?' Smith's response was immediate and deadly: he discharged both barrels of a double-barrelled shotgun into the vehicle. One of the shots struck sergeant Gibson on the face and head, the other struck Hope on the arms as he tried to shield his face. Campbell was able to get out of the car to arrest the gunman while Hope, although badly injured, made his way to the night porter at the County hotel to call for assistance. Meanwhile, a passing driver took the injured men to hospital but there was nothing that could be done to save Gibson who was pronounced dead.

Although born in Peeblesshire, Gibson's entire twenty-year career in the force had been spent in Dumfries and Galloway. And the town was horrified that such a well-known figure had been killed in the line of duty. He was the town's most popular bobby and was known affectionately to everyone who knew him as 'Big Bill'. The impact that the event had on Dumfries is not hard to imagine even to this day. More than a thousand people attended sergeant Gibson's funeral at St Michael's cemetery. It is a scene that one newspaper report painted with sombre sympathy:

> The streets in the town through which the funeral passed from Sergeant Gibson's home to St Michael's Cemetery were lined with citizens of the town, paying their last respects to one who was popular among all classes of the community and was held in high esteem by all. . . . The crowd was hushed to silence as the funeral procession moved slowly through the gates and up the central avenue.

One colleague said at the time:

> He very often tactfully turned an irate complainer into a friend of the 'polis' and sometimes a contributor to one of our funds of that day. He had always a cheery word for his old comrades and his passing came as a severe blow to all of us who knew him so well. His cap badge bore the words *Semper Vigilo* and we are proud to

> know that on his last tour of duty Willie lived up to the highest traditions of the force in which he served so ably and loyally, might not his epitaph be *Semper Fidelis*.

After an initial appearance in Dumfries Burgh Police Court before bailie Marchbank, Smith appeared at the High Court in Dumfries on 24 July 1951 charged with the murder of sergeant Gibson, the attempted murder of constable Hope and with stealing a shotgun and cartridges from his father. He pleaded not guilty to all three charges and also lodged a special plea that he was insane at the time the acts were perpetrated. Interest in the case was unprecedented: the court buildings in Buccleuch Street were packed as Doonhamers – mostly women, reported the *Daily Record* – queued to watch events unfold at the four-day trial. Some people even turned up as early as two in the morning to ensure they got a seat. This fascination was not a subject that the *Dumfries and Galloway Standard* of the day felt able to chastise its readers for:

> Interest in the trial was widespread and newspaper reports were read with avidity. Some people were inclined to take a superior attitude to the common interest and regard it as morbid, but we do not share that view. In a free society such as ours it is natural that people should be concerned about the safety and security of human life, and in the administration of the law. Possibly everyone who read the reports was an unofficial juror, and weighted the evidence with the same care as the fifteen who were empanelled. The fact that our courts are conducted with open doors and that any citizen may be called upon to act is the best guarantee that justice will be done without fear or favour.

The case itself was reported in enormous detail. One of the first witnesses was 25-year-old Andrew Smith, the brother of the accused. He testified that at one o'clock on the morning of the incident his brother had come into his bedroom, with a shotgun in his hand, and said: 'Get up. I have something for you to do.' Robert Smith then forced his younger brother to take dictation for two hours in an old jotter. One of the notes in the jotter read: 'When I go out of the door I am going to shoot the first policeman I see.' On the instructions of his brother, Andrew Smith then got dressed and they walked together to a phone box in Holm Avenue. Robert told Andrew to call the police and tell them there was a madman wandering around Troqueer with a shotgun.

Andrew Smith also said that although Robert drank heavily at weekends, he was quiet and normal. He stated that, to his knowledge, his brother bore no ill will towards the police. Then Robert Smith's father gave evidence to the effect that his son was level-headed with no particular grudge against the police. But he did acknowledge that he had tried, to no avail, to get him to cut down his drinking. And it was clear that drink had played a part in Smith's rampage: he admitted to police that – on the afternoon and evening before the murder – he had been drinking beer, whisky and brandy in various pubs. When the pubs closed in the afternoon he drank two bottles of wine and in the evening began another tour of the pubs. At the end of the night he had gone to the British Legion club for a nightcap. He said he was so drunk that he could not remember leaving the club.

Kenneth McDonald – his best friend – was next into the witness box. McDonald had been drinking with Smith on the night in question and said that later on, after he and his wife had gone to bed, Smith had come to his home at 93 Irish Street and forced him to write down the following statement at the point of a gun: 'I Robert Smith killed a man tonight. I held up K. McDonald and his wife and forced them to write this.' But, strangely, this incident took place *before* the shooting in Bank Street; McDonald told the court that he heard two shots after Smith had left his house. Alcohol had completely befuddled the mind of Robert Smith.

The evidence against Smith was compelling and his only chance of getting off was to prove that he was temporarily insane at the time of the shooting. But the evidence of Sir David Henderson, professor of psychiatry at Edinburgh University, undermined this line of defence. Henderson testified that he had examined the accused and found no sign of insanity. In summing up, it fell to his defence counsel – John Cameron KC, dean of the Faculty of Advocates – to try to save his life. While acknowledging that Smith fired the shot that killed sergeant Gibson, Cameron eloquently argued that a guilty verdict on the murder charge would be inappropriate:

> I am not asking for mercy, but only for justice because a just man is always a merciful one. I ask you to find that this young man is not to be branded as a reckless murderer of an innocent police officer, but as one who truly at the time was so rendered irresponsible by the onset of mental disease and therefore should be treated as one within that category or at least that the measure of his crime is not the awful and grave crime of murder but the lesser one of culpable homicide. I leave the life of Robert Dobie Smith in your hands. It is for you to hold it and weigh it and if you think fit to preserve it.

As the jury of five men and ten women retired to consider the evidence a crowd several hundred-strong gathered outside the courts in Buccleuch Street, anxious to hear the verdict. They did not have long to wait; the jury took just thirty-two minutes to come to its unanimous conclusion: Smith was guilty of the murder of sergeant Gibson and the attempted murder of constable Hope. As the foreman delivered the verdict, Kenneth McDonald slipped out of the courtroom and walked across the corridor to another room where the Smith family were waiting. When McDonald told them the news, Smith's father collapsed and his mother let out a piercing scream that was heard by everyone in the building, including her son.

The judge, Lord MacKay, had no option but to sentence the accused to death and as Smith stood up to hear his fate he was visibly shaking and had to hang on to the rails in the dock to steady himself. Lord MacKay, as he raised the black cap, said:

> Robert Dobie Smith, in view of the jury's finding the sentence upon you is that you be taken from this place to the prison of Dumfries and from there to the prison at Edinburgh where you will be detained until August 17 when between the hours of eight and ten in the morning within the prison you will suffer death by hanging which is pronounced for doom.

After losing an appeal, Robert Smith went to the gallows at Saughton prison in Edinburgh on 15 September 1951; it was the first execution in the capital since 1928.

But what were the reasons for an apparently rational man going off the rails with such devastating effect? The Smiths were said to be respectable, 'God-fearing' people with a tremendous pride in home and family; his father, a railwayman, was teetotal and did not allow drink in his house. And Robert Smith seemed to have led a perfectly normal life: he had been educated at St John's primary school and Dumfries Academy and, at the time of the killing, had a good job with an electrical contractor at the ICI plant at Drungans. He also had a commendable war record; during the Second World War he had served in a Royal Navy minesweeper with some distinction, being mentioned in despatches on several occasions.

Three factors emerged during the trial that provide clues to Robert Smith's motives. In the first place – and contrary to the evidence given by his father and brother – there was a degree of animosity towards the Dumfries constabulary. Just two months before the murder – in March 1951– Smith was lifted by a sergeant Dunn for being drunk and disorderly and taken to the police station for questioning. This incident had clearly preyed on his mind:

after he was told that he had killed sergeant Gibson, Smith replied: 'It is a pity it was not that bastard Duncan'. It was thought by detectives who interviewed him that he had mixed up the names 'Duncan' and 'Dunn'.

A second factor was personal tragedy. Anne McDonald – the wife of his close friend Kenneth McDonald – had a 2-year-old nephew, Alan Service. Smith was devoted to the boy and often played with him at the McDonalds' house. Then disaster struck: the child fell accidentally from a window and was killed instantly. The funeral was arranged for 22 May 1951, the day that Smith went on the rampage. One of the notes taken by his brother Andrew in the jotter makes Robert Smith's feelings crystal clear: 'The day they bury him is the day I expire.' He had also arranged for a wreath to be sent to the funeral with a card that read: 'To my wee pal, Alan'.

The third factor may have been the most important of all: love. Smith had gone out with a pretty 19-year-old waitress in late 1950 and she was clearly captivated by his dark and swarthy good looks; so much so that the couple became engaged after a short romance. The girl – Dumfries-born Joan Gillespie – was the sister of Anne McDonald, and the aunt of Alan Service. But Gillespie soon realised that he was not the man for her, as she later explained to the *Scottish Daily Express*: 'There was too big a difference in age between us. He took life too seriously and instead of going dancing with me he always wanted either to sit at home discussing books or films.' So Joan Gillespie broke off the engagement, which came as a devastating blow to Smith. Despite this he was determined to win her back and – to get in her good books – even travelled all the way to Glasgow to take dancing lessons.

But it was all to no avail. His dream of marrying the vivacious young woman was over. Her sister, Anne McDonald, believed that Smith thought 'he wasn't good enough for Joan and it played on his mind.' This was almost certainly the case on the fateful morning of

Anyone for cricket? A scene from bygone sporting days at St Joseph's College in 1941.

Social inclusion. The different classes mix happily side by side at the Rood Fair in the early part of the twentieth century.

A pram parts the typically massive crowds at the Rood Fair celebrations.

Guid Nychburris got off to a spectacular start in 1932 as this picture of the first Queen of the South, Louie Waland, and her entourage shows.

The unusual attractions offered by the fair on the Whitesands included the likes of Pearl the Oyster Girl.

The start of a whole new era. Dumfries High Street in turmoil as the controversial pedestrianisation process was in full flight.

The impressive façade of Dumfries Academy in 1897. The school has seen many famous pupils pass through its doors, including Jane Haining (inset) the 'Angel of Auschwitz'.

'A province of fairyland'. Doonhamers enjoy their Rood Fair festivities shortly before the outbreak of the First World War.

The Roaring Twenties. Girls step out to take a stroll through the 'shows' on the Whitesands.

A chain-driven lorry struggles to make its way through the dramatic floods of the river Nith around 1927.

Nith Place lives up to its name around 1910 as the waters spilled up towards the Mechanics Institute where the Loreburne shopping centre stands today.

Snowed under. The High Street fountain shows the dramatic depths of the snowfall of 1996, which briefly cut Dumfries off from the rest of Scotland.

The great playwright, Sir James (J. M.) Barrie (right) welcomes prime minister Ramsay MacDonald to Edinburgh University in 1932. Barrie, once a pupil at Dumfries Academy, was chancellor of the university.

(courtesy Empics)

John Laurie, born in Troqueer, became a star of stage and screen. He is best remembered today for his brilliant portrayal of private Frazer in the hit BBC comedy *Dad's Army*.
(courtesy Empics)

Cop killer: The murder that shocked Dumfries . . . and Scotland.
The murderer, Robert Dobie Smith, is in the middle.
Clockwise from top: the victim, sergeant William 'Big Bill' Gibson; Joan Gillespie, the girl who broke off her engagement to Smith; Alan Service, the 2-year-old whose death devastated Smith; Kenneth McDonald, the killer's best friend.
(artist's impression of Smith by Richard Phipps)

Billy 'Basher' Houliston, the hero of Wembley, and still the only Queen of the South player to represent Scotland while at Palmerston.

Two Queen of the South greats from different eras.

Jim Patterson,
who signed from Luncarty Juniors of Perthshire in season 1948/49 and went on to score 246 goals for Queens in his 14-year career at Palmerston.

Ted McMinn.
Nicknamed the 'Tin Man', the boy from Castle Douglas signed on in 1982. He was a true entertainer and one of Scottish football's genuine characters. McMinnn was later signed by Rangers for £100,000, a Palmerston record at the time.

(both courtesy of Ian McDowall)

Roy Henderson in action at Palmerston. For his performances between 1946 and 1957 fans voted him the greatest Queens player of all time in 2004. Despite his nickname – the 'Clown Prince' – Henderson was a formidable goalkeeper.
(courtesy of Ian McDowall)

Who's that with Allan McNish? Dumfries's fastest man in conversation with Jackie Stewart and Prince Andrew at the 2002 British Grand Prix.
(courtesy Mirrorpix)

Doonhamer Giancarlo Rinaldi takes a little inspiration from the most famous writer ever to inhabit the town, Robert Burns.
(David Henderson)

22 May 1951 and another note he dictated to his brother seems to confirm the psychological effect the break-up had on him: 'I think if I had married her I would have become an honest and useful citizen, but I am 30 and of no further use to this world.' We can never be certain about the workings of anyone's mind but unrequited love can often have a devastating effect on even the most rational among us.

10

MOVIE STARS

A small, sleepy, south-west Scotland town might be a long way from the glamorous world of motion pictures. Indeed, you could be tempted to think that Dumfries's closest link with the world of movies would be its proximity to the village of Holywood, which is just one letter short of its more famous namesake. But it has had more than its share of brushes with cinematic superstardom.

One of the first times the Queen of the South came into contact with the silver screen was for the shooting of the 1978 remake of John Buchan's classic novel, *The 39 Steps*. Originally filmed in the 1930s, the rerun was to star Robert Powell, one of the top British actors of the day. Much of it was filmed on location around the region and a number of locals played important roles either as extras or by assisting the production unit.

It is hard to imagine today but, in March 1978, Powell was at the peak of his popularity and his arrival created something of a stir. Just a year earlier he had starred as Jesus in a major television drama entitled *Jesus of Nazareth* and it turned out to be the biggest role of his career. Also a big name at the time was another cast member, the very glamorous Karen Dotrice, the child star of *Mary Poppins*. It must have been hard for Doonhamers to get their heads around the fact that the film crew was on location in the Ae forest.

Powell, producer Greg Smith and director Don Sharp were due to spend ten days filming in the region. The weather does not appear to have been particularly kind and the shoot broke off at one point to allow the star to be whisked off to Carlisle airport to attend the premiere of another of his films, *The Four Feathers*, before returning. Other locations used included Morton castle near Thornhill and the Castlemilk estate at Lockerbie.

Local people took on a wide range of tasks but Dumfries post-woman Pam Thomson surely had the most unusual. She looked after Robert and Babs Powell's baby, Barnaby, during filming and the *Standard* featured the story on its front page on 15 March 1978.

Other locals had a more concrete part to play in the production of the film. Doonhamer Bill Cunningham was involved in finding extras. Dumfries piper Ian Clowe was involved with a scene in the movie in which he piped cast members into Castlemilk House after a shooting party. And local actor Billy Jardine – famous in the town for many roles, particularly in panto at the Theatre Royal – landed a small speaking part as 'The Tramp'. Apparently the producers were so impressed by his acting skills that – on a day when rain made filming impossible – it was decided to write him into the movie. It was also a great boost for local amateur dramatics as many people got the chance to see at first hand how a motion picture was pieced together.

While most of the filming for *The 39 Steps* went on outside of the town, it was a very different proposition for the Tom Cruise blockbuster, *Mission Impossible,* almost twenty years later. It was one of those blink-and-you'll-miss-it roles for the town but nonetheless it had an impressive financial spin-off.

The filming took place in 1996 for a scene in which Cruise was to hang off the top of a train in the Kent countryside. Filmmakers could not find a straight piece of track in the English county and eventually discovered what they were looking for in the heart of Dumfries and Galloway, mostly in Nithsdale. It was ideal, with the track running through open countryside and few bridges or power lines overhead. The filming was done on the local railway line with the Hollywood star being superimposed later by modern technology.

The sight of an engine fitted with a couple of goods wagons trundling between Annan and New Cumnock became a common one, with the camera attached to front or rear and a helicopter filming from other angles. In the finished film, Tom Cruise and Jon Voight battle it out on the roof of the train as it speeds towards the Channel Tunnel. The only images of Dumfries and Galloway are of scenery flashing by in the background. The scene ends when the train and helicopter enter a tunnel in the thrilling climax to the movie.

Although Tom Cruise may not have set foot in Scotland, never mind in Dumfries, the spin-offs were important and underlined that the town and surrounding area could provide the infrastructure for a major motion picture. A film unit was based in Dumfries for about five weeks and spent around £125,000 in the local economy. Among the facilities used were a helicopter-landing site at the Crichton and a hospitality tent behind the Safeway store in Dumfries. And, of course, restaurants, bed and breakfasts and other local businesses benefited.

If that was a fleeting appearance for the town there was a more substantial role in the football movie, *The Cup*, later retitled *A Shot at Glory*. Robert Duvall was both star and producer and the other big names included former Rangers player Ally McCoist and Michael Keaton of *Batman* fame, although Keaton was not involved in the Dumfries filming. Duvall had been keen for some time to produce a soccer film and he flew into Scotland to shoot scenes for the fictional tale of Kilnockie Football Club, a tiny club that harboured the dream of reaching the Scottish Cup final.

'I first spoke to Queens chairman Norman Blount to tell him there was a major, Oscar-winning Hollywood star who wanted to make a film about Scottish football set in Scotland,' explained the region's film officer of the time, Kenny Eggo. 'At that stage I couldn't tell him who it was but Norman, to his credit, was really up for it and finished up getting a bit of the action.'

A series of photographs at Palmerston, Gretna and other small grounds across the region were taken with the aim of having the whole film shot in Dumfries and Galloway. During an eventful trip to Los Angeles, Mr Eggo knocked on plenty of doors and eventually delivered the photos to producer Rob Carliner and spoke to him on the phone. But then the lines of communication went quiet and it appeared the chance might be lost.

The first hint that Duvall – star of such blockbusters as *Apocalypse Now* and *The Godfather*, in which he played the role of *consigliere* to the Corleone family – would seriously consider Dumfries as a potential location came in May 1998. The American legend was in Scotland to soak up the atmosphere at the Scottish Cup final between Rangers and Hearts. During that time he was gently persuaded to take a detour via the south-west along with writer Denis O'Neill to see what the area could offer.

'I contacted Norman again to see if he was going to the Scottish Cup final,' said Mr Eggo. 'Duvall was coming over so we tried to arrange a meeting. I told them not to expect a long meeting – but we ended up spending about two hours with them. But somebody in Glasgow had told them it would take all day to get to Dumfries – we told them it was only an hour and half!'

The Dumfries delegation was heading home when the mobile phone rang in their car and it was Denis O'Neill – who boasts *The River Wild* on his film credits – to inform them that the movie's producers would visit Dumfries to check it out. By the time the men from Hollywood had met with the then Queen of the South managers Rowan Alexander and Mark Shanks and their players, and seen what Palmerston had to offer, they were clearly impressed. They left the town reassuring everyone that they would film at least part of the movie in Dumfries.

Once again, however, there was another lengthy period of silence. Changes at the production company left the film in limbo and it was unclear whether it would ever see the light of day. Even so, plenty of publicity was coming the town's way as stories kept surfacing over who might star in the film and where it might be shot. 'Queens would have had an enormous amount of coverage out of it anyway,' reckoned Mr Eggo. 'They were always mentioned in press coverage. Denis O'Neill was even talking about setting up a Queen of the South supporters club in Hollywood.'

Eventually, over a year later, the promises came good. In July 1999 director Michael Corrente and his team descended on the home of Queen of the South to capture scenes that would later make it to the silver screen. Unlike the *Mission Impossible* venture this time there was no major spend as the visit to Dumfries was much more fleeting. But in the space of a couple of days the town, the football club and local people could hardly have got a bigger boost.

The club reckoned that 7,000 locals packed the ground as extras for the day of filming. A number were lucky enough to be selected to play the part of Kilnockie fans and were paid a fee; the others in the ground were unpaid. Duvall told this author at the time of filming that he was delighted with the way things had gone:

> We knew things would be great here and that's the way they turned out. Norman Blount and Shirley Bell couldn't have done more. And the crowd were unbelievable. They didn't have to pay but it was still a great turnout. The club were excellent – they set the whole thing up and made it very easy for us.

The local council had decided to mock-up tickets for the fictitious quarter-final clash between Queen of the South and Kilnockie. And despite knowing their team would be knocked out in the interests of the script the Dumfries public turned out in force. They were treated to a long stint of filming as time and again the cameras tried to capture an incident or a goal from a particular angle. Yet spirits rarely flagged despite the length of time it took to record the scenes.

Among those to feature in a big way were the Dumfries and

Galloway constabulary pipe band and local radio broadcaster and raconteur Davie Shankland, who appeared as a radio commentator. Proceedings got under way at about 3 p.m. and took almost four hours to complete. During that time there was a surreal atmosphere in Palmerston park as movie men kept strolling out onto the pitch to interrupt the action and take events back thirty seconds to film them again. Eventually, according to plan, Kilnockie came out 3–2 winners and Palmerston's moment of movie fame was over – at least until the film came out.

'It had a big impact on Dumfries and Queen of the South,' said Mr Eggo. 'There was a film crew here for one day's filming. I don't think the spend was as big as it could have been but in terms of publicity it was definitely a successful project. And Queens were immortalised in film.'

It would be fair to say that the film met with mixed reviews, with Duvall's Scottish accent as Kilnockie manager Gordon McLeod getting a lot of stick. The lack of realism in the football scenes also came under fire. Still, most Doonhamers watching the movie were more interested to see if they, or their friends, appeared in the background. It was an interest that extended for some time as, after a premiere at the Toronto Film Festival in 2000, the film was screened locally at the Robert Burns centre and then released on DVD and video in the summer of 2004.

There was a far warmer critical welcome for the next production to come out of Dumfries, which was directed by a Scot, Peter Mullan. *The Magdalene Sisters* was an important film by any standards and its makers also spent a great deal of time in and around the town. The old Benedictine convent provided an ideal backdrop and a number of scenes were captured there by the crew when filming took place in 2001.

The producers spent three and a half weeks at the convent on Maxwell Street but also took in scenes in Moniaive and Kirkton among other sites. Initially there were fears that Dumfries might lose out to Ireland but Scotland was seen as a better place to film given the sensitive nature of the subject matter (which looked at the way so-called promiscuous young girls were treated in homes run by Catholic nuns). In April 2001, the *Sunday Times* reported that tax breaks were going to lure the Scottish film team to Ireland. The paper estimated that the boost to the local economy in Dumfries could be around £3 million but the film producers admitted that the 'Irish option had good financial incentives'.

Luckily Dumfries and Galloway Council pulled out all the stops to ensure that *The Magdalene Sisters* was filmed locally. *Rough Cuts* magazine reported that John Archer, chief executive of Scottish Screen, was delighted to have turned things around. 'These are very special circumstances,' he said. 'There was the prospect of a film which has had most of its funding from Britain going to shoot in Ireland. We didn't want that to happen. *Magdalene* also has the potential to give a boost to an area very badly affected by foot-and-mouth. We have done everything we can.'

'Financially we had to fight quite hard,' admitted Belle Doyle, film officer of Dumfries and Galloway Council, looking back at that time. 'But in practical terms it was the obvious choice with a convent owned by a private individual. Even though they found quite a few convents in Ireland they couldn't get permission to film.'

However much brinkmanship was involved there is no doubt that the outcome pleased all sides. A funding package put together by the council, local enterprise company and Scottish Screen ensured that the project went ahead. It was certainly worthwhile with an estimated spend of close to £1 million during filming. And, of course, the big-screen success put Dumfries on the movie map once again.

Producer Frances Higson was delighted with the location which Geraldine McEwan – who played the lead role of Sister Bridget – also relished: 'We've been filming down here for five weeks,' she said at the time. 'At the beginning of the film we were out and about. We were at Kirkton village hall, we were at various locations for the first week for the beginning of the film. Then we went to the convent and we were there for three and a half weeks. It's perfect in virtually every way and the owner has been brilliant with us, he's been really helpful.'

The local assistance obviously did the trick since the film, although controversial, was a critical and commercial hit. As well as being awarded the Golden Lion at the prestigious Venice film festival it also scooped the discovery award at the Toronto international film festival. And even three years after filming the movie was still getting all sorts of publicity and accolades. In 2004 it was in the running for more awards from the London Film Critics Awards and the Directors Guild of Great Britain. It simply underlined the importance of the film and the town was happy with a share of the glory. '*The Magdalene Sisters* remains a great showcase of how film-friendly this region is,' said Ms Doyle. 'The film is also a shining example of what a talented director can do with a tiny budget, not much time, and a cast that had a lot of unknown and inexperienced actors.'

The film critics also loved it and the following comments from *The Guardian* are fairly typical: 'This extraordinary film is celluloid incendiarism, rabble-rousing cinema with a delirious, delicious edge of black comedy which I estimate to be about 90–95 per cent intentional.'

But not everyone agreed with this assessment. The Catholic News Service was less sympathetic: 'Mullan puts forth an over-simplified worst-case scenario in which every nun is a monster and the only priest connected with the laundry has forced a simple young woman confined there to yield to his sexual demands.' Whatever people's opinion of the film it was one of the most talked-about releases of the year and gave Dumfries a reputation as a good place to make movies. *The Magdalene Sisters* was certainly a ground-breaking project as it was a first Scottish-Irish co-production. And the impact was both immediate and long term for the town as local film officer Ms Doyle explained. She said: 'They [the producers] spent just over half a million pounds while the filming was going on. That was in accommodation, food and paying local extras – that money was going straight into businesses in Dumfries. Then on top of that there was all the money going into night clubs, pubs and restaurants.' Much of the credit for this must go to the South-West Scotland Screen Commission, as without it movie producers may not have considered the town.

The Queen of the South was certainly acquiring quite a movie portfolio having passed for Kent, Ireland and, of course, her glorious self. That curriculum vitae was to stand her in good stead with another, small budget, movie that could not, in truth, have been filmed anywhere else. *Red Rose* was the first film on Robert Burns to be made in decades and was shot on location in Ayrshire and Dumfries and Galloway. It had its premiere at Ayr racecourse in 2004 and was another string to the town's bow. The rapid rise of Dumfries and Galloway as a potential film location shows no signs of slowing down and that can only be good for the area. Whatever the film, the town has proved it can put on anything from a cameo performance to a starring role.

11

SCHOOL DAYS

Nothing ever stays the same in the world of education. There is hardly a year that goes by when there is not a major change in the world of learning. Too many buildings, a shortage of property in the right places, the difficulties of recruiting and retaining staff – these have all hit Dumfries at one time or another. Throw in various revamps on how education should be delivered and it makes for an intriguing world.

The baby boom of the post-war years started to have an early effect as a nationwide shortage of teachers threatened to block admissions to some schools in the town. A report by the rector of Dumfries Academy at the time, Alfred Lodge, stated that he had seen the number of pupils at the school rise from 700 to 1,200 since 1931 'with a corresponding increase in the number and complexity of the problems to be solved'. The teachers' trade union, the Educational Institute of Scotland, highlighted its fears that the year ahead was going to be a difficult one with the prospect of teaching double classes.

One of the answers, at least in Dumfries and in the surrounding area, was an almost unprecedented school-building boom. In September 1951 the first part of the new High School at Marchmount was opened with 250 pupils coming in from the existing High School in George Street. 'Little wood has been used in the construction of the school,' reported the *Dumfries and Galloway Standard*, 'the main structure being of reinforced concrete with exterior walls of Locharbriggs sandstone and interior walls of brick.' The intention at the time was that the school would have an operating capacity of 850. As pupils moved from George Street to Marchmount a role had to be found for the town-centre site. A decision was made to focus on technical education at the old location with a special emphasis on motor engineering and electrical engineering.

Two years later came the Barony Farm school at Parkgate, a few miles outside the town. Some forty-five pupils started that first term in what was dubbed an 'experiment'; the idea being to teach pupils the rudiments of farming along with more conventional subjects. The old mansion house – once a prisoner-of-war camp – clearly did a good job since Barony has continued with its dual role to the present day.

Next to receive an educational boost was Lincluden where a new block containing eight classrooms, assembly hall and general purposes room was opened in 1955 by Dumfriesshire MP, major Niall McPherson. There was a significant move in Troqueer in 1958 when the new primary school was officially opened by ex-provost Thomas Bell. The cost of the project – designed to accommodate a maximum of 340 pupils on the site – came in at just under £60,000. One of the main reasons for building the school was the growth of Maxwelltown as a residential area. The extension of the burgh boundaries in 1948 had also increased pressure on school rolls in the area.

By the 1960s the trend for construction still showed no signs of slowing. In 1960 the new £120,000 extension to St Joseph's College was unveiled by Bishop McGee. The building contained four science labs as well as extra dormitories and an assembly hall. Just twelve months later the £485,000 project and 13-year-long wait to construct Dumfries High School was declared complete with a school roll soaring to over 1,000. The school had been only part-occupied as it had suffered from a six-year delay between 1951 and 1957 before funding became available for the second phase. It would appear the wait was worthwhile according to reports of the time: 'From the outside the impression is a favourable one,' said one, 'austerity has been done away with and there is brightness everywhere.'

With all this expenditure it was little wonder that the education committee heard in 1963 that their costs had soared to a record £2 million per year and were likely to continue to increase for the next decade in the view of county convener Sir Arthur Duncan. Nevertheless, the early 1960s saw continued expansion as a new primary school was opened in Lochside in 1960 and got its 'official' opening two years later – as the two-phase project drew to a close at a cost of £126,000. Four years on – in 1966 – there was another school for the area when St Ninian's primary was opened by the provost, Ernest Robertson. He told teachers and pupils: 'This is another stage in making Lochside not simply an outlying housing scheme but a community in its own right, having its own schools, shops and churches.'

To that end plans came forward at the end of the 1960s for a secondary school in Lochside as well. But few could have forecast the bitter debate that would ensue over the name. The choice was between Lochside High School and Maxwelltown High School – in the end councillors opted for the latter by a couple of votes. Bailies Beck and Webb tried to fight off attempts by old Maxwelltonians to 'annex' the name of a school situated outside that historical area. Mr Beck argued that he could not see where the name Maxwelltown had any association with the area at all. But the words of another councillor, Alfred Turley, clearly held sway. He noted it was thirty-nine years since Dumfries and Maxwelltown had merged and a lot of people on the Maxwelltown side of the water still resented it. And he successfully argued that if the burgh – which effectively died nearly four decades before – had still been around the new school would have been part of it. And so, by thirteen votes to eleven, Maxwelltown was agreed and the first phase was completed by 1970.

This was part of the council's controversial two-tier educational system, under which pupils attended either Dumfries High or Maxwelltown High for the first two years of secondary school. Then the more academically inclined would be skimmed off to Dumfries Academy to complete their education. By 1975 there were already moves afoot to scrap this system and make all four Dumfries secondary schools – Maxwelltown High, Dumfries High, Dumfries Academy and St Joseph's – into all-through schools providing the full six years of education. This too, however, proved difficult to achieve as the costs were great and a certain stigma had been created during the two-tier era.

It was not just about Lochside, however, as Heathhall was soon the subject of a major development of its own with £1.2 million earmarked for the construction of the new technical college. Work got under way in 1972. Nobody could say things had moved at a hectic pace since the need for this kind of development had been highlighted back in 1966. Two years later the council had bought a twenty-acre site for the facility, which was to include workshops, labs, classrooms, administration block, dining hall and kitchen.

These new educational establishments in the new centres of population inevitably meant closures elsewhere and by 1978 Dumfries and Galloway Regional Council headed the list of applications for closures with twenty-five accepted from 1975. But the closure policy often caused fury among parents in outlying areas. As budgets became restricted the days of the provision of new schools appeared to be over.

While some school closures were planned, and perhaps reluctantly accepted by communities, there was a bombshell in April 1982 that caught education officials on the hop. The Benedictine convent, which had provided both primary and secondary education for Catholic girls, announced that it was facing closure unless the local authority intervened. The council found a solution by absorbing pupils into other primaries and the older girls into St Joseph's

College. The problem was blamed on the death of the headmistress, Mother Monica, which left the nuns unable to continue running the school. Whatever the reason was it came as a shock to parents, pupils and teachers. The convent had been founded almost a century earlier and although there had been rumours the previous year that the council had been approached to take it over there was little preparation for the event.

If the closure of the convent was one of the most dramatic in the town's history it did confirm the trend to rationalise the number of school buildings. This was always likely to stir up anger among parents as happened in the mid-1990s when a hit-list of six schools appeared in the papers. The initial closure process was started but subsequently shelved. Still, it was only delaying the inevitable as authorities realised that something had to be done to repair crumbling buildings. Instead of singling out particular schools it was decided a more wide-ranging consultation was required to decide the shape of things to come and, perhaps, attract private finance to help tackle the backlog of repairs.

The Public Private Partnership (PPP) proved to be one of the most contentious issues of the day as it brought private money into education. A side effect was that some schools were closed and others merged. Consultants were brought in but their proposals for closure were thought to be too severe. By January 2002 a figure of around eighteen closures was settled on with new buildings and major repairs being the enticement for parents to agree to the plans. In Dumfries, the main items on the agenda were plans for a new Roman Catholic school to replace St Teresa's and St Andrew's, a new school for Heathhall on the outskirts of town and the possible closure of Maxwelltown High and Dumfries Academy to create a new secondary. Also initially targeted for closure was Brownhall primary but local parents were among many dotted across Dumfries and Galloway who mounted strong campaigns against the proposals.

By October of that year it was already recognised that the

options being proposed for Dumfries were the most contentious. The education committee chairman of the time, Tommy Sloan, accepted as much. He said:

> The Dumfries issue is certainly causing a lot of controversy but one thing we are clear about is that in the new outline business plan there is flexibility built in to allow for every scenario that the full and, I've no doubt, lengthy consultations will throw up. PPP is not just about closing schools, it's not just about building a handful of new schools, it's about revamping every single school within Dumfries and Galloway to bring every school up to the school of the future standard.

That may well have been true but parents, pupils and teachers did not see it that way. A number of protests were mounted at Dumfries and Galloway Council headquarters in Dumfries and throughout the area as consultation meetings took place. The public, it seemed, wanted new schools but did not believe the price of losing the old schools was one worth paying. In the face of public outcry the council started to back down from the original closure position.

Indeed, by October 2003 Dumfries MP Russell Brown accused the council of wasting two years and causing a lot of unnecessary stress when he claimed only one school would close under the PPP project. He commented: 'They have subjected many parents and local communities to undue worry about the future of their local schools and wasted thousands of pounds of taxpayers' money on pointless consultant's reports and local people are left asking just what was the point of this exercise?' He claimed that Beattock was the only school left that might still close. His claims were dismissed by education bosses but just the same it did appear that from an original proposal of eighteen the number of schools to close was going to be fairly small.

Among the most controversial suggestions was the possible

closure of one of the four Dumfries secondary schools. Concerns surfaced, particularly among Dumfries Academy parents, pupils and friends, since this was seen as the most prominent site with the greatest potential for either redevelopment or sale. Understandably there was a great deal of play made of the school's achievements and its importance in the history of the town. A number of fiery meetings were held before the authority eventually decided not to include any secondary closures in their plans. Despite repeated rumours of its demise this also meant a reprieve for Maxwelltown High School. There was a degree of disappointment from councillors and the director of education, Fraser Sanderson, that a more innovative approach could not be taken. He said: 'I'm a bit disappointed in the report myself – I would have loved to be coming forward saying, "let's open a new school". But I simply found I couldn't justify that.'

By 2004 there was still some confusion about the future shape of education in Dumfries, even if it was certain that the four secondary schools – Dumfries High, Maxwelltown High, St Joseph's College and Dumfries Academy – would stay open. A new primary at Heathhall remained on the wish list while the only closures were to be St Andrew's and St Teresa's, which would be replaced by a new Catholic primary. But parents at St Theresa's were still carrying on their fight in March 2004 by seeking a judicial review and taking their case to the Scottish Executive. Even the proposed site for the new school seemed to be called into question on the basis of expense with a number of options still being explored.

One thing is for sure, however, there will be no shortage of controversy when the subject is education. It has long been a sensitive subject and even in politically apathetic times still provokes an outcry. More and more innovative approaches have been made to find the funding to both upgrade current buildings and, ideally, build new schools. It has been clear over the years that Dumfries and Galloway has done a pretty good job in maintaining academic standards despite increasing financial pressures. Over the years the pendulum has swung back and forward between growth and contraction. The priority, of course, is to provide the best facilities for young Doonhamers to get all they can from their schooldays so they can match the achievements of some of the famous names who have preceded them.

12

CLASS ACTS

A school will always be more than bricks and mortar. Every educational establishment there ever was has looked with justifiable pride on the achievements of its pupils and remembered fondly its favourite teachers. Dumfries is no exception having seen countless famous names pass through the doors of its secondary schools and had some formidable figures in charge.

Dumfries Academy is rightly proud of its connection with J. M. Barrie, of *Peter Pan* fame, while St Joseph's boasts of its literary qualities through former pupil A. J. Cronin, author of many fine novels including *The Citadel* (1937) and *The Keys of the Kingdom* (1942). A qualified medical practitioner, Cronin wrote extensively about the lives of doctors and, in the 1960s, the very popular *Dr Finlay's Casebook*, adapted from his books, was produced for both radio and television.

To flip back through the pages of any Dumfries secondary is to come across a range of intriguing characters that have lit up the scene both at school and beyond. Some may be remembered more fondly than others but few are forgotten. One student whose remarkable story deserves to be retold to a greater audience is Dumfries Academy's Jane Haining, who began her studies at the school in 1909. Born in Dunscore in 1897 she lost her mother as a child and acquired a steely determination that was to steer her career path later in life. She became dux of the Academy and worked in a thread maker's in Paisley for a decade but when she heard about the Church of Scotland Jewish Missions in the 1930s she reportedly declared: 'I have found my life work.'

By 1932 she was in charge of a home for girls in Budapest with 400 children in her care, most of them Jews. Many at the mission were orphans but there were others who had been sent by parents who knew of the outstanding education provided by the Scots. What struck everyone who met the young woman was her profound care for the children, and this shone through in her letters home. She was clearly touched by the tragic cases that presented themselves to her on a regular basis. She wrote: 'We have one new little six-year-old, an orphan without a mother or a father. She is such a pathetic wee soul to look at and I fear, poor lamb, has not been in too good surroundings before she came to us . . . she certainly does look as though she needs heaps and heaps of love.'

It was a love that Haining freely gave throughout her time at the mission but it was to face the sternest possible test when the Second World War began. Although she was home on leave when war broke out – and the church offered to let her stay there as the conflict escalated – she decided to go back and carry on her work. 'If these children need me in the days of sunshine, how much more do they need me in the days of darkness?' she reasoned.

During the war years her work became more and more dangerous as the threat of Nazi invasion grew. Eventually, that moment came in 1944 and while missionaries were ordered home, Haining opted to stay and do what she could to help 'her' children. She did everything in her power to protect them but the pressure on the mission grew increasingly intense as the occupation continued.

It was at the beginning of May that the events she must have dreaded – and yet partly expected – started to unfold. An SS raid of her office and bedroom gave her just moments to gather a few belongings and prepare to leave. An array of charges were levelled against her including espionage, helping Jews and, bizarrely, weeping as she sewed the yellow badges onto the clothes of some of her children. For these 'crimes' she was transported first to prison and then to the concentration camp at Auschwitz where she met her death in the gas chamber a couple of months later. It is thought she died on 16 August 1944, at the age of forty-seven and by then she was known simply by the number allocated to her by the Nazis: 79467. She was one of more than one million killed in the camp in the space of just three months. Her children were devastated as one said years later: 'I still feel the tears in my eyes and hear in my ears the siren of the Gestapo motor car. I see the smile on her face while she bade me farewell. . . . The body of Miss Haining is dead, but she is not alone, because her smile, voice and face are still in my heart.'

It is still believed that she was the only Scot to be executed in Auschwitz. Because she was a British citizen an 'official' death certificate was sent back to Scotland claiming that, after being arrested for espionage, she had died in hospital of 'cachexia brought on by intestinal catarrh'. The truth was far more tragic and terrible. She had paid for her love and dedication to the children of the mission with her life.

Haining's life and work have not gone unrecognised in either her homeland of south-west Scotland or further afield. Her name can be found on the memorial on the Academy gates more than sixty years after her death. There are tributes in both the Queen's Park church in Glasgow and the church at Dunscore. Some fifty-three years after her death she was also awarded a medal and a place in the Righteous Among the Nations at Yad Vashem, the Holocaust Martyrs and Heroes Memorial. The award was received by her sister at a ceremony in Glasgow.

But these are small signs of recognition for such an amazing woman and it is little wonder that even in the twenty-first century many believe that the former Academy pupil deserves closer attention. Villagers in Dunscore were keen to see a more lasting and significant memorial made. They wanted to see her name added to the local war memorial and also intended to launch a fund to erect a permanent statue in her memory. Contacts were being made in 2004 to determine if the Royal British Legion would consider adding her name to the memorial.

It is little wonder that such a dramatic tale has attracted the attention of filmmakers and, in 2005, it emerged that plans were in the pipeline to produce a film about her life. The film is provisionally entitled *There are mountains on the road to heaven*, and derives from her own words in a letter home. The intention is to recognise the woman the screenwriter dubbed 'Scotland's Schindler' after Oskar Schindler, the German industrialist who saved many Jews from the death camps. The film, backed by the European Commission, Scottish Television and Scottish Screen is to be based on interviews with four surviving pupils of the school in Budapest. One of them recalled: 'I remember her as a wonderful light in that dark period. She created an atmosphere of democracy, equality, tolerance and we all felt incredibly privileged as it was such a contrast with the world around us.' There is little doubt that such a poignant tale would lend itself perfectly to the silver screen and would be a deserved tribute to a remarkable woman. Dumfries rarely shouts about the achievements of its own and yet this is surely a case where her story should be taught to every local child, and told proudly to anyone who cares to enquire about our most famous sons and daughters.

From an educational point of view another important figure at the Dumfries secondary, judging by the tribute paid to him in the Academy yearbook of the early 1950s, was John Gall. He spent over thirty years at the school as deputy rector and principal teacher of science between 1919 and 1952. During that time hundreds of pupils must have come under his bespectacled gaze. Having completed his war service in the First World War he was appointed to the maths and science department before taking on the deputy rector role in 1936, in which capacity he played a large part in the daily life of the school. The rector paid him a moving tribute on his retirement:

> The bare record can, however, give no picture of the rectitude and integrity with which his duties have been performed, and of the affection with which he is regarded by all who worked with him or were taught by him. Rectitude and integrity, probably quite erroneously, are frequently associated with aloofness and lack of warmth. No greater mistake could be made if this were the impression of John Gall conveyed by these words. His is of a warm-hearted and friendly nature, and his final qualities are the result of his personal knowledge of human failings and the self-discipline which has moulded his character into what we now so greatly revere and respect.

His contribution to the school must have been significant but he was overtaken, in years of service at least, by his colleague Margaret Williams who amassed thirty-seven years as a teacher at the Academy between 1929 and her retirement in 1966 – in other words, her entire career. As well as working with four different heads of department she ran the languages department for a spell during the Second World War. From 1951 onwards she also held the post of woman adviser, which must have required considerable understanding of young people's problems. She received significant praise at the end of her days at the Dumfries school and tribute was paid by head girl Lesley Beaton in the school book. She wrote:

> Her invaluable counsel on the day-to-day problems of school life has been constantly sought, and countless numbers of pupils are indebted to Miss Williams for her wise advice and kindly assistance. We record our gratitude for her unobtrusive yet indispensable help with the organisation which has ensured the success of so many school functions, and regard it a privilege to have known and worked with her.

The post Second World war period produced less dramatic times for students and teachers alike with the threat of conflict now gone but one of the most memorable years – for a variety of reasons – must have been 1956. Both St Joseph's and the Academy saw the death of a famous leader while there was also a sporting triumph.

A road accident caused the death of rector Alfred Lodge, who was a major figure in the history of Dumfries Academy for a quarter of a century. Born in Feltham, Middlesex in 1893 he was a headmaster in Lancashire before he was appointed to his post at the Academy in 1931, a position he held until his death. Not surprisingly the school magazine of the year carried a poignant tribute to him and praised the way he led the school 'guiding its destiny with wisdom and foresight at a period of transition and expansion'. He was also highly thought of in educational circles and received the Fellowship of the Educational Institute of Scotland in 1954. Among the other offices he held were president of the Rotary Club, master of the Guild of Players, chairman of the municipal orchestra and Grand Master Mason of Dumfriesshire. His major passion, according to the tributes paid by the school, was music and this showed in his involvement with the school choirs and orchestras. Pupils and staff were among those present at his funeral in St John's Episcopal church in the town to pay their respects.

One appreciation summed him up in this way:

> Jealously guarding and encouraging among us that spirit of loyalty and service which he considered to be the very life blood of a successful school, his aim was to have pupils leave Dumfries Academy conscious of what was most desirable in our traditions so that they could play their part in shaping for good the unknown future lying ahead.

At almost exactly the same time St Joseph's College was also in mourning for the loss of Brother Joseph Benedict. He had been the principal for twelve years and made a lasting impression on the school. Although he was no longer in post when he died there were many who still remembered him. The boys had paid an emotional tribute to Brother Joseph when he retired and it was reprinted in the *Blue Book* of 1956 to sum up how pupils had felt about him:

> If we may stress one of your qualities above the others it is this, the kindliness and sympathy we have always found from you. Our new boys know it in their early days of home-sickness: others know it in their everyday difficulties: but above all, we Seniors have experienced it in the wise help you have given.

Happily it was not all bad news for the town's secondary schools that year as the Academy clinched the Scottish Secondary Schools Shield by beating Bellahouston of Glasgow, the reigning champions, in the final at Hampden Park. The match report from the school magazine makes intriguing reading and gives details of the chants for the favourites that greeted the Doonhamers on their trip to Glasgow. 'It reminded us that Bellahouston were favourites to retain the Shield; and that we were the outsiders, a team from the backwoods of Scottish Schools football.'

Things started badly as Bellahouston went ahead within ten minutes but then the Doonhamers got into their stride, as the match report in the Dumfries Academy school magazine noted:

> The strength and purpose of Riddell and Drainer now began to emerge as the dominant features of the game. Walker and Barclay at last found the measure of their opponents more dangerous wing, and never again relaxed their hard-tackling grip. Ballantyne settled to his usual strong forceful game. . . . The equalising goal, just before half-time, was an entirely individual contribution from Currie – a fierce right-foot shot from a free-kick outside the penalty area.

With the wind at their backs in the second half the Academy boys took control, with forwards Bell and Currie, wingers Jaap and G. Little and centre W. Little pulling the strings. It was Jaap and G. Little who found the net to give the Dumfries side a seemingly unassailable lead of 3–1. 'With a two goal lead we settled down to give an exhibition of football that was almost Continental in its cheeky intricacies,' said the school's match report. But the Academy was pegged back when Bellahouston hit back and the pressure built on the defence until G. Little struck again. Although there was a consolation penalty late in the game, Dumfries Academy held on for a historic win by four goals to three. 'We left the stadium as we entered it – to the sound of "Two! Four! Six! Eight!" – but this time the words had an unmistakably borrowed air, and the voices a lusty Palmerstonian inflection.'

A few years later on St Joseph's was to know sporting achievement at the very highest level through one of its pupils. Former student Jim Brogan was part of the Celtic squad during one of the most successful periods in its history. His career with the Bhoys started as a teenager in 1962 but it was only after their European Cup triumph of 1967 – the first team in Britain to lift the trophy – that the former College boy really made his mark as a defender. From 1969 to 1975 he was a regular with the Parkhead side and helped them to countless glories along the way before transferring to Coventry City towards the end of his playing days. Among his most famous games were the European Cup final of 1970, which the Glasgow giants lost to Feyenoord and also the infamous semi-final of the same competition against Atletico Madrid. During Brogan's spell at the club the team collected almost every major trophy on offer, including the Scottish league title nine times in a row from 1966 to 1974, the Scottish Cup seven times, the League Cup six times as well as their European heroics.

This was, of course, carrying on long-established links between the school and the club. Indeed Celtic's founder, Brother Walfrid, is buried in the grounds of St Joseph's and high-ranking members of the club were regular visitors to the school throughout the 1950s and 1960s. In fact one of the most influential men in Celtic's history was also a pupil at St Joseph's – Sir Robert Kelly, who was chairman of the club from 1947 until the 1970s and took the momentous decision to bring back former player Jock Stein as manager in 1965. Kelly's Celtic roots were deep: his father, James Kelly, was captain of the first Celtic team in 1888 and later became chairman. Robert Kelly was clearly proud of his association with St Joseph's; he even named his Glasgow home 'Marisdale' in honour of the Marist brothers who ran the school.

Another sportsman in a very different field was the adventurer Jock Wishart, a pupil of Dumfries Academy. It seemed there was no challenge that he could not rise to, and he became recognised as an expert in the field of polar expeditions and all sorts of energy-sapping and weather-defying challenges.

The first time he hit the headlines was in 1992 when he was part of the team that walked unsupported to the geomagnetic North Pole. That feat in itself might have been enough for most people but not for the hardy Doonhamer. Instead, he headed there again four years later as part of the first televised trek to the magnetic pole.

Those icy adventures captured the imagination of thousands across the globe but particularly in his home town where the North Pole seemed a world away from the quiet streets. One of his next challenges was to undertake the incredible task of rowing across the Atlantic as part of a 1997 race. Along with team-mate Duncan Nicoll – in their boat the *Mount Gay Rum Runner* – they finished eleventh in a little over sixty-three days of gruelling action. It was an event full of high drama and no little risk to life as early in the race high winds blew many of the competitors more than 100 miles off course while others were forced to call for help from passing ships, which meant disqualification. The two brave rowers completed the course and arrived exhausted but ready for their next challenge.

Again most nine-to-five workers might have been happy with that achievement but there was to be another attempt at a record by Wishart soon afterwards. This time he was project leader as the *Cable and Wireless Adventurer* attempted to circumnavigate the globe in record time, and in less than the eighty days of Jules Verne's classic novel. This they achieved in a little under seventy-five days, beating the old record held by the US submarine *Triton*. Leaving Gibraltar in 1998 the team set out on the incredible 26,000-mile journey in their 115-foot monohull boat. The team called at fifteen ports en route before making it back to Gibraltar in good time to beat the record.

And by 2003 Wishart's adventurous streak still showed no sign of letting up as he was involved in organising and supporting teams taking part in the incredible Polar Race, whose organisers dubbed it, with some justification, as the world's toughest race. Competitors were expected to fend for themselves in temperatures as low as minus 40 degrees centigrade while hauling a 70-kilogram sledge over 350 miles through icy waters, avoiding open water and, of course, polar bears. Wishart admitted: 'Those who finish the Polar Race, which is expected to last thirty days, will have completed a race which is probably the world's toughest.'

The new millennium is likely to produce many more inspiring characters among both pupils and teachers in Dumfries. But 2004 was also the end of an era at one Dumfries secondary when Brother Cyril, for so long associated with St Joseph's College, passed away. His time as a teacher and long involvement with the past-pupils' association made him one of the best known figures of the many brothers to be involved with the school. But soon after his death it became clear that a long-standing link with the town was about to be severed. The last Marist brothers moved out of their base in Dumfries in the same year bringing to an end their connections with the town. The links had been in decline since the school came under the control of the local education department in the 1980s but the departure of the Marists was still a significant change for St Joseph's.

Whatever the future may hold for education in Dumfries, the past has shown that it is likely to feature some intriguing figures that will make their mark in the most diverse of fields. There is something interesting about people who come from a small town and go on to make an impression on the world stage. And playing a role in their formation will be school staff, teachers and head teachers who watch over their early years. There have been any number of larger-than-life characters passing on their wisdom to Doonhamers in years gone by and that shows no sign of letting up in the years to come.

13

STAR QUALITY

Nobody ever got a big head living in Dumfries. Like any small town or village it has a way of cutting its sons and daughters down to size if they think they have grown too famous for their home town. 'Ah mind o' you when you wur a wee lad' is almost inevitably foll-owed by some embarrassing story. At the same time Doonhamers are intensely proud of people from their neck of the woods who make a name for themselves. We can claim a link with a diverse range of high achievers: from the author of the greatest children's story ever written to a Le Mans 24-hour winner, from a sitcom superstar to one of the top men in telescopes. Throw in a lead singer with a world-famous band that has been on the go for decades and you get a pretty mixed bunch. No matter what, we are proud to remind them of their Dumfries heritage and, by and large, they are happy to recall it.

A prime figure on the list of great Doonhamers is, of course, technically speaking, not a Doonhamer at all. But the Dumfries links of *Peter Pan* author J. M. Barrie are undeniable. Not only did he attend Dumfries Academy but he also lived in Victoria Terrace and it is widely accepted that the town provided the inspiration for his most famous character. Playing as a child at the back of the Moat Brae building was as close to Never Land as could be found.

To do justice to Barrie would take a book in itself and there are plenty dedicated to the subject. He began his writing life as a journ-alist and short-story writer before turning to novels, which included the highly successful *The Little Minister*, published in 1891. He later devoted himself entirely to plays, which brought him considerable critical and commercial success. In fact, the stage version of *The Little Minister* earned him £90,000 between 1897 and 1898, an enormous sum at that time. This was followed by other popular plays including *The Admirable Crichton,* first performed in 1902.

But his best known and most successful work was yet to come, and it is worth restating the part that Dumfries played in its creation. James Matthew Barrie was born in Kirriemuir in 1860 but in the 1870s he undertook his schooling at Dumfries Academy. The man himself admitted that the Moat Brae gardens in George Street – next to the river Nith and behind the school buildings – gave him the idea for *Peter Pan.*

'When the shades of night began to fall, certain young mathematicians chanced their skins, crept up walls and down trees, and became pirates in a sort of Odyssey that was afterwards to become the play of *Peter Pan,*' he said in a speech made in Dumfries years later. 'For our escapades in a certain Dumfries garden, which is enchanted land to me, were certainly the genesis of that nefarious work.'

And so it was that on 27 December 1904 his play, *Peter Pan,* had its first night at the Duke of York's theatre in London. One hundred years on it retains its popularity as witnessed by the release of lavish new versions of the story. For Christmas 2003 Jeremy Sumpter starred as the little boy who never grew up in the film directed by P. J. Hogan. Then, in 2004, a stunning cast list was assembled for *Finding Neverland,* telling the story of Barrie's creation of his most famous character. Johnny Depp, Kate Winslet, Dustin Hoffman and Julie Christie were among the stars for this tale of how Pan was born and how his success affected the life of Barrie and those around him. Such was the impact made by *Finding Neverland* that it was nominated for a best-film Oscar in 2005.

Perhaps the greatest shame for Dumfries is that little has been done to commemorate the spot where such a globally recognised figure was born. A small statue of Peter Pan in the gardens and a plaque in Victoria Terrace are about all that mark Barrie's links to the town. There were plans for a theme hotel to be located near the site of the Peter Pan garden but, as of early 2005, nothing had been done about them. Instead, concerns persisted about vandalism at the Moat Brae building, which was used until recently as a residential home but has now fallen into disrepair.

Another famous pupil of Dumfries Academy was also to find fame in the fickle world of theatre. John Laurie was born at 3 Ryedale Terrace in Troqueer on 25 March 1897, the son of a mill worker, William Laurie, and his wife, Jessie Anne Brown. He went on to achieve great success in more than 150 plays but will always stick in the minds of television viewers as private Frazer in the BBC situation comedy *Dad's Army*.

Laurie did not set out to be an actor; he trained as an architect until the outbreak of the First World War in 1914. After he was invalided out of the army he eventually took the momentous decision to tread the boards, a decision based largely on his love of Shakespeare. It proved to be a wise move as he appeared in many Shakespeare plays at the Old Vic theatre in London, covering most of the major parts the Bard had to offer. His London debut was in 1922 and despite offers from film producers he seemed content with a stage career.

Eventually he was tempted from the theatre by a part in the first film version of *The 39 Steps*, directed by Alfred Hitchcock and starring Robert Donat. Coincidentally, a remake of the movie, starring Robert Powell, would be shot in his home town some years later. It turned out to be another astute career move and Laurie's performance was highly praised by the critics in what turned out to be one of the best British films of all time. Following this success he carved out a niche in a huge number of movies in the years that followed. Among his roles were Blind Pew in Disney's *Treasure Island* (1950) and parts in Laurence Olivier's versions of *Hamlet*, *Henry V* and *Richard III*.

He appeared in some major British movies of the time including Alfred Hitchcock's first 'talkie', *Juno and the Peacock.* Laurie also starred in *The Edge of the World* for Michael Powell in 1937, which told the tale of the last days of an island community. *Bonnie Prince Charlie* (1948) with David Niven was generally rated as a bit of a disaster. While tales of the shipyards were captured in *Floodtide* (1949), in which he played alongside fellow Scots Gordon Jackson and Jimmy Logan. He worked with David Lean on *Madeleine* and his final film role was in a remake of the *Prisoner of Zenda*, which was filmed just a couple of years before his death.

Ironically, it was when he was considering retirement that he landed the role that made him a household name. *Dad's Army* was the story of the Local Defence Volunteers of Walmington-on-Sea and Laurie played private Frazer, the town's undertaker, a man who saw the downside in every situation. He was seventy-one when the first series hit the screens, in black and white, in 1968. But those six episodes were enough to ensure a longevity that few in the cast ever dreamed would stretch to eighty-three episodes and nine series until it finished in 1977. By that time the pessimistic catchphrase – 'We're doomed!' – uttered by Frazer in nearly every episode had entered into popular usage.

The series was a massive hit and a film version was made in 1971 in which Laurie starred and also a stage musical in 1975, which the Doonhamer was not involved with. Along with the likes of captain Mainwaring, sergeant Wilson and corporal Jones, the Frazer character became so well-known that Laurie was among six cast members who made a guest appearance on the *Morecambe and Wise Show* in 1971. Even repeats of the show years later could still pull in seven million viewers. And Laurie was a key element in that great example of ensemble acting. When he died in 1980, just a few years after the end of the television series, his place among the great comic actors – indeed great actors – was assured.

Paying tribute to Laurie's talents, his long-time accompanist during his stage tours, Claire Liddell, told *Scottish Field* magazine in 1984: 'John's on-stage personality was magnetic and he had the gift of communicating by some mysterious osmosis, a certain electric adrenaline to his fellow artists.' And although he lived much of his life in England, Laurie never lost a fondness for his homeland. He and his sister owned a cottage on the banks of the Nith and he told a special *Dad's Army* magazine why the place was still so important to him:

> When I'm in that place, I have the feeling that I've come home. It's a part of the world that hasn't been spoilt by the passing years. It's a good place for honest men. You will find no honour for the prophet there. Occasionally, one of my old friends will say, 'I saw you on television the other day, John.' There will be a long pause and then maybe he'll say, 'Ye were alright'. That's the highest praise I can ever expect up there. And that's the way I like it.

If Barrie and Laurie both became household names this was not the case for another prominent Doonhamer. Although many will never have heard of Robert Waland his work in a specialist field made him world renowned. He deserves his place among any list of the great and good of Dumfries in modern times.

Born in the town's Leafield Road on 15 September 1908 he was educated at St Michael's and, briefly, at Noblehill school, before attending Dumfries Academy. For much of his early years he earned a living as a travelling lemonade salesman around Dumfries and Galloway and in Ayrshire. Yet, in a way typical of the British genius for invention, he spent his spare time honing his love of telescopes – a field in which he rose to great prominence.

One tale which sums up the young man's determination to succeed, despite the difficulties placed in his path, is how he photographed a total eclipse of the sun as a 19-year-old in Glencaple. Having constructed a seven-and-a-half feet solar camera at home he cycled with it and his two brothers, Goodwin and Frank, to

Richmond in Yorkshire. This was a trip of over 100 miles yet they found the energy to get up at three in the morning to position their camera to capture the event. Although clouds played havoc with their attempts they still captured images of the eclipse.

Waland's skills served his country well during the Second World War when he worked as a precision engineer, initially in Glasgow and later at the Heathhall airfield with the Royal Air Force. It was shortly after the war was over that his efforts finally got the recognition they deserved. Having constructed an amazing telescope at his uncle's house – Orlington in Rotchell Road – it was inspected by a passing professor of astronomy at St Andrew's University. He was so impressed by the Doonhamer's work that he was immediately offered the post of assistant research associate at St Andrew's, an opportunity he seized with both hands.

If the Waland story up to that point had been that of the enthusiastic amateur, he blossomed in the academic world. Working in tandem with Professor Erwin Finlay Freundlich he played a huge part in the construction of a telescope which, by 1952, was able to afford scientists at St Andrew's the possibility of photographing the stars with a clarity that had never before been achieved. Waland had already carved himself a major niche in the world of astronomy. His amazing achievements prompted Freundlich to say, after working on another project together: 'Yes, Waland is a genius. Without him I could not have started on such an ambitious enterprise. Without him, this whole thing would have been impossible.'

This glowing tribute and the work he was carrying out brought Waland to the attention of astronomers everywhere. In the early 1960s the Dumfries man was swept away to the University of Arizona in Tucson where they required assistance with one of the first telescopes financed by the National Aeronautics and Space Administration (NASA) for planetary research. This work was completed in the summer of 1965, and was once again hailed by experts in the field as an amazing advance.

Later, Waland helped build a telescope designed to carry out asteroid research while his earlier work was used to take thousands of detailed pictures of Jupiter. This incredible instrument also took photographs of the moon, which were used in one of the most important books of the time on lunar studies. On his retirement from practical work in 1976, the Doonhamer was presented with one of these hefty tomes to mark the occasion. His book, *Optics of the Cassegrain Telescope*, is recognised as one of the foremost works in this important area of science. Although Waland is no longer with us, his legacy in astronomy is assured.

In more modern times, Doonhamers still hit the headlines for a variety of reasons but none have made a greater impact in the world of sport than racing driver Allan McNish. Born at Cresswell maternity hospital in 1969 he was clearly destined to be involved in motor sport from a very early age: he was six times Scottish champion and three times British champion in the world of karting during his school days at St Andrew's primary school and St Joseph's College.

He rapidly rose through the motor-racing ranks with stints in Formula 3 and Formula 3000 before knocking on the door of Formula One as a test driver with the McLaren team in 1990. Incredibly, it was a love affair that would be put on hold for more than a decade as test roles with Benetton and Toyota eventually led to a full grand prix season in 2002 with the Japanese outfit. In between times, however, the Doonhamer captured one of the most prestigious crowns in the sport.

Ventures into *gran turismo* (GT) racing were proving more and more successful for McNish, who was in demand and had secured a seat with Porsche, one of the top teams. In 1998 – along with team-mates Laurent Aiello and Stephane Ortelli – he was ready for a crack at the gruelling Le Mans 24-hour endurance race. Until a couple of hours from the finish, McNish and his two colleagues seemed destined for second place but gearbox problems in the Toyota leading the race provided an opportunity that the flying

Doonhamer was happy to accept. After completing 352 laps of the 13.6-kilometre circuit he took the chequered flag in front of an estimated crowd of 250,000. He later described, with typical modesty, his thoughts on the triumph: 'With an hour to go on Sunday I stepped into the car not expecting to win. We were expecting to be second but the intention was to push the Toyota as much as possible and put him under severe pressure and hope that he got problems – and he did. To be involved in the history of Le Mans is absolutely tremendous and it is also Porsche's fiftieth anniversary. It is a tremendous day for me and for the team. When I stepped on to the podium it was a shock to see so many people and a very touching experience. It's a feeling that I don't think you could repeat in any type of race.'

McNish went on to finally get the Formula One drive his talents deserved in 2002 when Toyota returned to the sport. The car was never truly competitive, although the Dumfries driver regularly impressed with his cool control. When he was dropped after just one season, McNish became a popular pundit on ITV's Formula One programmes. After being long linked with a possible return to Formula One in 2004, the Doonhamer instead opted for a return to the Le Mans series, which brought immediate results with a triumph in the 12-hour Sebring race. And in the summer of 2004 he had another tilt at Le Mans but crashed out. Typical of the man and his character is his determination to return to Le Mans in 2005.

In the equally glitzy world of pop music, Dumfries can also stake a claim to a top performer. Stepping up to lead singer with a band that has been around for almost thirty years would be a daunting prospect for anyone. But it is one that Ray Wilson, born in Troqueer in 1968, took to in some style with Genesis.

The Dumfries singer had already enjoyed some measure of chart success in 1994 when his band Stiltskin enjoyed a monster hit with the single 'Inside', which went to number one and was part of a highly successful advertising campaign of the day. But when that group split it could have been the end of the road for Wilson's career. Instead, he got a shot at one of the biggest gigs in the game when Phil Collins quit Genesis, a band that had been on the go since 1967 and had already survived the defection of another lead singer, Peter Gabriel, in 1975. So Wilson was following in some illustrious footsteps when he took the job in 1997.

Apparently, the other band members had heard his voice on the Stiltskin album and likened it to Gabriel's voice on their early work. Band member Mike Rutherford said at the time: 'We listened to hundreds of tapes and Ray's voice really stood out. It had a quality that really moved me. His voice is thicker and harks back to early Genesis.'

After a first audition, Wilson was called back and a few weeks later was offered the job and jumped at the chance. His first album with Genesis, *Calling All Stations*, was followed by a major tour in which he and the band played to huge crowds. The Doonhamer took it all in his stride: 'It's a buzz playing in front of a big crowd,' he told the *Standard*. 'My most frightening experience was playing the White Hart in Dumfries years ago when there were only 25 people in the place.'

Unfortunately, album sales in America were disappointing and the band decided not to continue with Wilson in the lead-singer role but it had taken his work to a new audience. After working with Genesis he released another album with the band Cut, while his solo album, *Change*, came out in 2003. The world of rock and roll has been a tricky one for the Dumfries artist but a string of prominent collaborations and the strength of his solo work mean that he could be a major force for some time to come.

There have been many other Doonhamers who have made a major mark over the years and it is hoped there will be many more to come. Whatever they achieve they can be sure that their home town will be watching them with pride – just as long as they don't ever get too big headed!

14

THE UNUSUAL UNIVERSITY

There can be few places of learning with a stranger story to tell than the Crichton campus. Originally intended as a home for education, it was used for decades as an asylum. Yet more than a century and a half on from its creation, the Dumfries site was eventually to revert to a role far closer to that originally envisaged when several seats of learning joined forces to create a new model for higher education in its graceful grounds.

The story of Elizabeth Crichton, widow of Dr James Crichton, is relatively well known. In 1829 she intended to use money left by her husband to follow his wishes, which were 'to appropriate by far the large proportion of the Residue of his Fortune in Founding and Endowing a College at Dumfries'. But the plans suffered a number of setbacks and were eventually rejected by the government of the day, one reason being the number of unfilled places in the Scottish universities at that time.

So it was back to the drawing board for Mrs Crichton and, by 1833, when the plans for a university were formally abandoned, she decided to dedicate part of her fund to the founding of a 'Lunatic Asylum' to house up to 100 patients. A woman with such drive and determination was not to be denied and in 1839 the Crichton Institution for Lunatics opened its doors to patients. The announcement in the *Shipping and Mercantile Gazette* promised a separate bedroom for each 'Pauper Patient' while 'higher grade' patients would enjoy 'handsomely furnished rooms, or suites of rooms, to which are attached baths, douches, etc, galleries and balconies overlooking the town and vicinity'.

Over the years a farm, artesian well, church, electricity station, laundry, climatology station, gardens and the impressive Easterbrook Hall sprung up on the site along with a number of large 'Houses'. As treatments became more sophisticated the Crichton adapted but, by the end of the twentieth century, it was becoming clear that there was less need for the facility. Moves towards care-in-the-community had seen the number of patients using the Crichton fall while demand was growing for a university facility in Dumfries. At long last, and more than a century after her death, Elizabeth Crichton's original idea had started to take shape.

Throughout the 1980s and into the early 1990s pressure had grown for higher-education provision in Dumfries. The rapid growth in the number of institutions being granted university status gave hope to its proponents. It appeared improbable that any existing establishment in the town could be converted into a university. So the first hurdles to overcome were finding a site and attracting supporters.

The plans took a major step forward in 1995 when Dumfries and Galloway Regional Council made the bold move of buying the Crichton Royal site in a complex £23 million sale-and-lease-back scheme. The council was concerned at the thought of the buildings being sold-off piecemeal and snapped up the land – which had been declared surplus to NHS requirements – but left the administration to the newly formed Crichton Trust. Although the deal was pushed through – to meet a government deadline of 31 March – there was initially no clear vision of how the site might be developed. 'The purchase leaves a number of questions unanswered, principally what will happen to the site,' reported the *Standard*. 'Although previously discussed options have not been ruled out, the likelihood of a university being developed is at best many years off. The possibility of relocation for the headquarters of the new unitary authority has been ruled out and housing development is not a favoured option. Officials were vague about the future but seem to see, initially at least, business being attracted to the existing buildings.'

If there was no clear vision, momentum for a higher-education campus grew quickly. One of the people who clearly saw the opportunity was retired educationalist Dr Joyce Minton of Moffat, a long-standing campaigner for a University of Southern Scotland. Within a few days of the Crichton deal being sealed she was part of the group that launched a committee to campaign for the creation of a university in the town. Its hand was strengthened by the growth in the number of such establishments across Scotland: from four in the years before the Second World War to thirteen by the mid 1990s, yet the closest to Dumfries was about eighty miles away. The time had come, it was reasoned, to plug that gap.

'Up to now money has flowed away from this region in the form of student grants and income to the benefit of other regions, but, more importantly, talent has flown away never to return,' argued Dr Minton. And she underlined the importance of fulfilling Elizabeth Crichton's original wish for the site: 'It is an investment, not an expense, otherwise other areas would not be so anxious to retain the benefits in their hands. We simply want a more even distribution of these resources.'

There were those who were sceptical that the plan would ever come to fruition but there was growing support for a new facility. The opportunity was not going to slip away and one of the country's leading educationalists, Sir Graham Hills, outlined a way forward in May 1996.

He argued that it would be unproductive for the Crichton to attempt to compete with established universities like Edinburgh or Glasgow. And, in any event, the cost of establishing a fully independent university was put at a staggering £100 million. As funding on this scale was unlikely to be forthcoming it was suggested that Dumfries should pursue a less traditional model with the emphasis on teaching rather than research. In that way not only could the university take up a pioneering role but would also be more likely to attract financial backing. One of the key proposals was to offer a more broad-based degree than other institutions. In that way the Crichton could become an institution with its own unique qualities rather than competing for the same students as other universities. The Internet revolution was also crucial, allowing access to information in a rural setting.

This was the concept that the project, more or less, decided to adopt. By the summer of 1996, the dream of a Dumfries campus came a step closer when the University of Glasgow was confirmed as a major player. It unveiled plans to establish a college in the town with a target of 600 students. The lead role of the University of Glasgow not only made the plans more credible but also offered the prospect of a standalone institution if the demand was there. The University of Glasgow was happy to let Dumfries University walk before it could run.

'Our interest derives from our long involvement with Dumfries and Galloway,' explained the principal of the University of Glasgow, professor Sir Graeme Davies. 'Many of our students come from the area and we have provided the region with extra-mural continuing education for many years. We have identified a real opportunity to create a higher education presence in Dumfries and reinforce the university's traditional links with the area.'

The intention was for the first students to be on site by October 1998 but that plan had to be put on hold in September 1997 due to a delay in a government announcement on higher-education policy. Without the guarantee of funding there was no way the Dumfries scheme could go ahead. So a delay of a year was agreed, with September 1999 pencilled-in for the first influx of students.

Nonetheless, 1997 did bring a boost for the campus with the news that Dumfries and Galloway College had secured a lease on Maxwell House. A seven-year contract was signed with the Crichton

Development Company, which was designed to allow much of the college's degree provision to switch to the Crichton in May of the following year. The college had been working closely with the University of Paisley for a number of years providing courses in business, health and engineering, amongst other subjects. So another piece of the jigsaw had fallen into place.

Eventually, in 1999, the first students at the Crichton College of the University of Glasgow became educational pioneers at the new-style campus. Loosely based on an American approach to education the idea was to move studies forward under the banner of 'liberal arts'. It was also hoped to reach out to as wide a section of the community as possible: around forty people were to attend a summer school with the prospect that a good number of them would go on to study for a degree. The aim was to be accessible to all, as project director Morven Easton explained at the time: 'The whole degree is flexible and, where possible, we will be flexible in what we can offer and how we can offer it to suit individual students.'

By July 2002 the University of Glasgow section of the campus was ready to award the first degrees to its students. It was a historic day as five Master of Arts graduates received their honours in the impressive surroundings of the Crichton Memorial church. With many of their fellow students electing to carry on to a fourth year of study it was clear that the new institution was proving a success.

And in October of the same year around 150 students were part of a record-breaking intake. According to the director, professor Rex Taylor, it was a sign of how well things were progressing: 'We have met our target and we're delighted,' he said at the time. 'Not only have we achieved the overall numbers but we're attracting more students from further afield.' New entrants for the year included students from Kenya, the Republic of Ireland and increasing numbers from south of the border. They joined exchange students from the likes of Spain, France, Germany and the Czech Republic, helping to add to the cosmopolitan feel of the area.

But while things were progressing well for the four organisations on the site – Glasgow and Paisley universities, Bell College and Dumfries and Galloway College – it was not all good news. In January 2003 came confirmation that there would be no additional funding from the Scottish Executive, which had initially backed the project to the tune of £1.8 million. Education minister Iain Gray confirmed: 'The Crichton gains from the experience and traditions of a very diverse group of further and higher education institutions, but its funding depends on the priority and flexibility that the partners are willing and able to offer. I look to the partner institutions to maintain the commitment they have shown and to build the Crichton campus' position within the sector.'

Despite this setback the new institution continued to innovate, with the development of the Crichton University Scholarship Agreement. It allowed fifth and sixth year pupils at local schools to commit themselves to study there. And there was more good news in April 2003 when the first Bell College graduates in Dumfries picked up their honours at a graduation ceremony on campus.

All of this expansion did not come without a cost, part of which was an increase in traffic. A study of the road network of south Dumfries got under way to look at ways of improving the situation. And a proposal was made to the Scottish Executive for a sum of £30 million to build a southern bypass.

Contributing to this situation was not only the growth in educational provision – which now included the Barony College and the Open University – but also the growth in business on the site. It was predicted in 2003 that the number of jobs on the campus and the business park would rocket from around 800 to 2,500. And that figure was forecast to hit around 5,000 in the longer term. A figure of 1,200 was put on the number of students studying and around thirty companies had found a home there. Council convener Andrew Campbell welcomed this shot in the arm for the local economy. He said: 'The Crichton University Campus and Business Park is going from strength to strength in terms of growth in the number of students and new jobs. The transformation and development of the site has brought significant benefits to Dumfries and Galloway and further employment growth is predicted.' There was a further boost in 2004 when a new lease was signed for the site. It was predicted this would lead to further investment, on top of the £25 million that had already been spent.

On the cards was an ambitious revamp for the Easterbrook Hall, enabling it to become a major conference centre. Although still an impressive building it needed significant investment to bring it up to modern standards. Elsewhere a state-of-the-art library was proposed for the old laundry building. With the growth in the number of institutions on the campus, and the rapid increase in the number of students, it was clear that facilities needed to be enhanced.

Proposals were also being studied in 2004 to look at the possibility of setting up a land art centre on the campus, particularly to showcase the works of local artists Andy Goldsworthy and Charles Jencks. Studies had shown that a similar centre in Cornwall had generated significant income for the local economy (around £16 million) and there was a desire to tap into that potential at Crichton. All of which made the future look very exciting.

There can be few more unusual, but ultimately satisfying, stories than how the original vision for the Crichton was finally realised after almost two hundred years. For generations the beautiful grounds were home to some of the most unfortunate souls in society. But changes in patterns of care opened up the opportunity to develop the site in line with its original vision. The result was probably the most significant development in Dumfries for generations. The door was opened for business investment and high-quality further education. And situated on one of the most picturesque sites in the country the new campus will help to attract more people to the town and create an excitement so often said to be absent from the sleepy south-west. If Elizabeth Crichton could see it now she would rightly be proud. Her statue, unveiled on site by Prince Charles in 2000, is a fitting tribute to a visionary.

15

TRAVEL TROUBLES

Anyone who has ever travelled around Dumfries will know the headaches that parking and traffic have inflicted on the Queen of the South. The increase in the number of cars has caused a range of problems and an equally interesting range of solutions – some more successful than others. It would be true to say that none has come without its share of controversy.

By the late 1960s it was clear that something had to be done to sort out the congestion in certain parts of the town. High Street, Nith Place, Bank Street and Irish Street were among the areas of concern due to the level of parking and proposals were put forward in 1967 to clear them of cars, at least in part. The moves got a mixed reaction but people in the Bank Street area in particular had been campaigning for them for a number of years. The town council – planning twenty years ahead – then hatched its most controversial proposal: to remove traffic from the town centre altogether.

A meeting in Steel Avenue told the good people of Dumfries that they would be living in the most advanced town in Great Britain within twenty years: 'Dumfries will be a modern town,' said one speaker. 'There will be no traffic in the centre, only pedestrians, and private developers will be invited to construct the necessary modern buildings.' Although it was to take some time, the plans have come to fruition.

The arrival of traffic wardens in 1967 served to underline the problems. Six were drafted in to help the traffic flow, although there seems to have been some confusion over their role. In their first week of operation a police spokesman said that everything was going smoothly – but had to point out to the public that it was not actually the job of the wardens to find drivers a parking space!

More room was being made with the construction of the dual carriageway on Glasgow Road, which the council hoped would ease some of the headaches. This helped but the rising level of car ownership meant that planners were always swimming against the tide.

The trouble facing the town grew in the 1970s as cuts in public transport in rural areas started to hit deep and made car ownership almost a necessity. In 1971 Western SMT unveiled plans to cut losses on some routes, which would leave parts of the region with only a sporadic bus service. Then the paying customer faced an increase in costs as prices were 'rounded up' when decimalisation came in the same year. 'It is scandalous,' said one passenger. 'I am now having to pay 1*s*. 7*d*. for the fare that was 1*s*. 3*d*. last week.'

But the biggest earthquake was to come in the 1980s when a decision was taken to pedestrianise the centre; a decision that had been forecast twenty years earlier. The outline for the £1.1 million scheme was unveiled in the summer of 1987 and seems to have met with approval at that time. Out of 404 consultation documents sent out to those affected only 76 were returned, with just one being entirely against the plans. But if businesses and locals were happy with the plans they changed their tune when work actually started.

The first phase hit Friars Vennel in January 1988 and letters went out to shopkeepers on the thorny issue of disruption. A spokesman for the council pledged: 'Disruption of the normal activity in the Vennel will be kept to a minimum throughout the three months which the work will take to complete. Work will be phased to ensure that half the road width will be open at any one time, although the narrowest sections of the Vennel will have to be closed from time to time.' Judging by the outcry from traders in the area it is hard to believe that they felt the disruption was minimal.

'Vennel Obstacle Course', 'Ghostly Outlook for the Vennel' and 'Row Flares in Friars Vennel' were just some of the headlines of the time. Businesses in the area reported a slump in trade of anything up to 50 per cent. It is interesting to note that many of the shop-keepers interviewed about the effect on their business were no longer in trading at those premises about a decade and a half later. Michael Webb of the Gift Box dubbed the move 'absolute chaos for the whole Vennel'; Nasim Akhtar of the Jeans Centre reckoned it was a 'waste of money'; at Pets Pantry, Ken Wilkinson doubted whether he could win trade back; Margaret Wolstenholme of the Magpie gift shop said it was almost impossible for people to get into her premises; while George Munn of the Victoria Inn raised concern about restrictions on delivery times. Of these stores only the pub was still trading fifteen years on from pedestrianisation. Even those shops more upbeat about the move have closed. Lui Fusco, of Fusco's café, hoped that the works might lead to the 'rebirth of the Vennel' and Dorothy Wise of Newall's toy shop was aiming for a grand relaunch of the street once pedestrianisation ended. Other shops quoted at the time that had disappeared by the start of the twenty-first century included William Welsh the ironmonger, which had been in the area for decades, just like Thomas Hamilton the shoemaker.

Even when the work was over in the Vennel the controversy did not end. In one famous incident a pensioner slipped and fell on the new surface and threatened to sue the council. The elderly lady was rushed to Dumfries infirmary in May 1988 when she broke her hip on a sloping section of the new road. Another woman tripped on the surface a few days later and commented: 'One literally takes one's life in one's hands when shopping there.' Wheelchair users too highlighted problems with the sloping pavements, which the regional council agreed to address in future parts of the pedestrian-isation plan.

Still, at least the grand opening of the street gave some respite to the negative publicity. The Vennel's oldest resident, Dorothy Marshall, cut the ribbon on the historic day at the end of May 1988. Shopkeepers like Jim Higgins of Seton fishmongers were happy to be moving into the Vennel. He said at the time: 'I am confident that the new look will improve the number of pedestrians using the street and it is encouraging to see other shops improving their frontage as well.'

But the optimism of opening day quickly turned to disillusionment when people became aware of the poor quality of the workmanship. By July even the council was unhappy with the standard of the Vennel after its upheaval. So much so that payments for the work were held back. 'It's fair to say the finished article of the Vennel does not come up to expectation,' said councillor John Forteath. 'In particular the Celtic Cross, which was meant to be the highlight, has been highlighted for all the wrong reasons. Its cobbles, I believe, are second hand and brought from Ayrshire.' Roads boss Hugh Murray confirmed that the council would not be paying for the works until it was happy with them.

The lessons from the Vennel were not learned when the main redevelopment phase got under way in the town centre. Councillor Ronnie Jardine raised concerns in early 1989 about the difficulties faced by emergency vehicles in the town centre: 'At times more than a mile can be added onto a journey into the town to miss roadworks and other things which are going on,' he warned. But by April the town centre was deserted as traffic was stopped and the works got under way on the main phase of pedestrianisation. Unfortunately, it appears to have received the same reception as the Vennel works.

More than half the shops in the town reported a slump in trade and the head of the Dumfries shopkeepers' association, Douglas Barbour, sought an urgent meeting with council chief executive Neil McIntosh. 'The planning is too ambitious for our town,' he said at the time. 'The pedestrianised area is bigger than Buchanan Street and Glasgow has one million people to call on.' The biggest problem was parking with spaces – which had previously been in front of stores – now shifted some distance away. The manager of the town centre Wimpy, Marian Main, described the impact as 'disastrous'. She told one reporter: 'Our teatime and evening trade is practically non-existent.' While another High Street trader, J. Kerr Little the butcher, pleaded for the plans to be amended. He said: 'We are all saying moderate the plans, don't foist this great monster upon us. Dumfries can't cope with it.' Wimpy and Kerr Little's shop both disappeared from the town centre in the years following pedestrianisation.

Dumfries and Galloway Regional Council defended the plans. Councillor John Forteath assured angry traders they would see the benefits in the long run. He insisted the measure had wide support. He said at the time: 'It was not a fancy idea dreamed up by officials. It was the result of public consultation.' And he found some support among traders who were fed up of their colleagues talking down Dumfries. Their fear was that negative comment might have as much impact as parking troubles and turn Dumfries into a ghost town.

Public perception was probably not helped by the start of repair work on the Vennel project late in 1989 but it would be fair to say the final reaction was mixed. By Christmas the works were over and some stores reported record returns. 'The best Christmas ever' said Martin Corbett of ironmongers Andrew Rankin. 'I'm sure the new pedestrian precinct has had a lot to do with it.' While Cecil Johnston at Littlewoods – on the other side of the High Street – was equally pleased. He commented: 'We have had a record-breaking season and I'm sure pedestrianisation has played a part. Shoppers have stayed in town this year instead of travelling elsewhere.' And figures released by the council showed that 90 per cent of people approved of the plans. But some reservations remained as was highlighted by fears the following year that vandalism was being encouraged. The lack of traffic circulating at night was blamed and the continuing works provided easy material for vandals, it was claimed. By then, of course, there was no going back.

In the years since pedestrianisation there have been regular calls for the work to be reversed and cars allowed into the town centre again but none ever had any serious chance of success. Nevertheless, concerns persisted about the lack of atmosphere in the town centre after five o'clock and various measures were suggested to make the area more welcoming. There is no doubting that pedestrianisation transformed the heart of Dumfries but in a few years time something else came along that had an equally dramatic effect on the way people moved around the town.

The SCOOT system sounded like an ideal solution to Dumfries's traffic headaches. An increase in the number of cars coming into the town had placed pressure on an infrastructure that had not been designed to cope with the age of mass car ownership. There was growing frustration at the length of time drivers were spending stuck at traffic lights. The radical plan was to bring in more traffic lights; these would be 'intelligent' lights that allowed for a better flow. Unfortunately, the lessons of pedestrianisation were never learned.

The situation reached its nadir in 2003 when plans were proposed to improve traffic flow at the St Michael Street roundabout by replacing it with traffic lights. Everyone in the town had become acutely aware of the need to introduce measures to help cope with developments on the Crichton site, as well as hospital traffic and new housing on the south side of Dumfries. Not everybody agreed, however, that the use of further traffic lights was the answer but by March the work was ready to start. A council spokesman explained how the new system would work:

> Initially, the timings will be set manually to best suit the traffic patterns and then gradually the timings will be set automatically depending on actual levels of traffic. This process takes time, especially at a busy location such as this and the signals may tem-

> porarily be switched off while adjustments are made. We appreciate drivers have had to suffer delays as the works have been built but we would ask them again to be patient as the final phase is completed.

Unfortunately, the delays experienced in the build-up to the lights being unveiled were nothing compared to the trouble that followed when they were switched on. Drivers reported lengthy tailbacks and even at times when there was no traffic it seemed that waiting times were considerable. Such were the teething problems that the lights remained on for barely two days.

By May it had become clear that the traffic lights were an expensive mistake and they were never switched back on after the disastrous introduction. Councillors agreed to ditch the lights for a different system that incorporated a roundabout with other road improvements to help improve access. Some were more scathing than others in their criticism of what had happened.

'This has been a real PR disaster,' insisted the Conservative group leader Allan Wright. 'What we are finishing up with could have been met for a fraction of the cost.' And he even found some agreement from the other end of the political spectrum with a Labour councillor, George McBurnie, commenting: 'I think we now need a full review of the systems in Dumfries as people are criticising this council over it.'

The conundrum remained a difficult one for the town throughout 2003 and into 2004 with traffic levels simply too great for the old infrastructure to cope with. In an attempt to deal with the headache the council decided to ask the public for its views in a traffic survey in 2004 but even that backfired. This particularly related to access to south Dumfries where new development had caused more problems. The survey hoped to find out what routes drivers used and how demand could be eased at peak times.

Unfortunately, the timing of the census and its location led to problems. When the people distributing questionnaires were moved to Buccleuch Street bridge it led to tailbacks right along the street and piled up problems onto Glasgow Street. It caused many commuters to be late for work and the census was withdrawn. The aim of the scheme was laudable but it had been poorly executed.

No easy solution to the town's traffic problems had been found by 2005 but there is a determination to find a more co-ordinated approach. The concept of build first, and deal with the consequences later, was dealt a major blow by the St Michael Street lights' debacle. Of course, Dumfries does not have anything like the problems of a big city when it comes to traffic. But try explaining that to a motorist stuck in a lengthy queue along Glasgow Street and you will be unlikely to find much tolerance.

16

WHITEOUT

One thing that attracts and frustrates Doonhamers in equal measure is the climate. On the one hand they know they are unlikely to be subject to the meteorological extremes experienced in other parts of the globe but at the same time it can get pretty boring trying to find new terms to describe a wet and windy day. A bit like Eskimos with snow they have developed dozens of different terms to replace the word 'rain'.

All that changed for a brief spell at the beginning of 1996 when the town was visited by a weather front normally reserved for Alaska or Siberia. In the words of one tabloid, Dumfries became *Dum-freeze* as the snow started to fall and just kept on falling. It was reckoned to be the worst winter weather in at least five decades and prompted the declaration of a state of emergency. Not something that commonly occurs in Dumfries and Galloway.

What made the feet-deep blanket of snow all the more dramatic was that it appeared to arrive unannounced. The forecasts anticipated snow but nothing could prepare the town and its surroundings for drifts ten-feet deep. There was a dramatic silence about what was witnessed in an unbelievable spell of extreme weather.

The first flakes appeared on Monday, 5 February 1996 and then just kept on coming. For most of Dumfries what started as another day at the office quickly developed into something much more dramatic. It rapidly became clear that the snow was not going to stop; in fact, it intensified. Within a few hours it was obvious that anyone who had come to work in the morning faced a fairly stark decision – head home now or you will not get home at all. Indeed, conditions became so treacherous so quickly that even people trying to go a couple of miles were forced to abandon their cars at street corners and complete their epic journey on foot. By Tuesday morning the snow was stacked so high that most homes had it packed at least halfway up their front door and even getting to the end of the driveway involved a mammoth effort.

At one stage all roads in and out of the region were closed, adding to the siege mentality. Thousands of motorists were left stranded on motorways and side roads as conditions had rapidly deteriorated. Emergency centres were set up to cope with people caught out by the snow. Little wonder that by Tuesday afternoon a state of emergency was declared and secretary of state for Scotland, Michael Forsyth, offered the help of the army to try to shovel the region out of its predicament.

Dumfries and Galloway Regional Council marshalled its forces in their 'bunker' in English Street as they came to terms with the scale of the problem. More than twenty-four hours of constant snow had left schools closed, roads blocked, people stranded and businesses shut down. Not surprisingly they took up the offer of any help they could get. The type of help needed was explained by council chief executive Ian Smith in an interview with the *Standard*:

> We have called for military assistance. We need the use of their four-wheel vehicles to bring food out to places where people are stranded. The main problem is not clearing the snow, however, but getting snow ploughs past the abandoned vehicles. The region's main arterial routes are beginning to become passable but it only takes one lorry to break down to cause problems again.

With no pupils getting through many schools were used as emergency centres to cope with the sheer numbers of people who had been stranded. One of the main centres was set up at Dumfries Academy where hundreds sought refuge. Sprawled across the main hall in the school building they created a scene that was more akin to some war-torn country rather than the heart of rural Dumfries and Galloway. Many had just been passing through the region when they were caught by the unexpected turn in the weather. Others had set off for what they thought would be an ordinary day at work and were never able to make it home. Weather experts reckoned it was the worst the region had seen in fifty years. Douglas Yule of Weather Watchers in Laurieston confirmed just how serious the situation actually was:

> It's probably the worst snow since 1946. It seems to vary but the average seems to be about two feet with drifts up to ten feet. The region is basically buried in snow. The M74 is a disaster area. We have had reports of about 3,000 people stuck with many stranded in their vehicles overnight. The A75 and A76 were closed overnight. The only route out of the region that is passable without problems is the A77 from Stranraer to Girvan.

As well as snarling up almost every road across the region there were also problems for thousands of homes as the electricity network failed to cope with the calamitous conditions. It was estimated that 11,000 homes were without power at the peak of the crisis. Many battled for days to get power back as Scottish Power struggled with five sub-stations out of commission. Overnight between the Monday and Tuesday the company was unable to take any action as the number of homes affected started to mount. Normally they would have used helicopters to help pinpoint problem areas but even they were unable to operate because of the weather conditions. A spokesman for the company admitted at the time: 'These are probably the worst conditions for about 50 years and, although we are doing our best, it is very difficult.' Many families experienced a long, cold wait for power to be restored even as conditions improved.

Later in the week power chiefs were able to call in help from the army. Army helicopters carried engineers to the areas where work was most urgently needed and they were able to patch up the network. And while the majority of the people originally cut off were back on the grid by Wednesday other homes had lost their supply, leaving hundreds still in the dark.

The feeling of isolation was exacerbated as nothing seemed to be moving into or out of the town. Everything went on hold – on the Tuesday in particular – as forecasters predicted that more snow could be on the way. Royal Mail bosses sent staff home from their Dumfries office after the police advised trucks from the main sorting office in Carlisle not to attempt the treacherous trip up the A75. While at Dumfries infirmary non-emergency operations were cancelled as staff struggled to make it to work. And the large volume of phone calls put the hospital's main switchboard under such pressure that the public was asked only to call in cases of emergency.

There was a huge workload, too, for the people manning the region's gritters and snow ploughs. More than eighty men were working flat out for Dumfries and Galloway Regional Council's commercial group as they fought for two days to get the M74 re-opened and tried to clear up other roads. Divisional manager Ronnie Dempster commented: 'These are by far the worst conditions anyone has worked in for years. Our team is extremely professional but they are working at knockout pace to try to clear the roads. . . . It is quite harrowing at times. The snow is the worst ever and drifting has added to the problems.'

Factories across the town reported many workers braving the weather to keep the wheels of industry moving. At the ICI in Dumfries less than half the workforce was able to get to work but that was still enough to keep their Melinex lines operational. While at Gates Rubber Company in Heathhall the company was operating with a skeleton staff made up mostly of people who were within walking distance of the factory. The nuclear power station at Chapelcross in Annan used four-wheel-drive vehicles to help get staff from Dumfries and other towns across the region into work to monitor the plant's installations.

In the heart of Dumfries there was a surreal atmosphere by the Tuesday morning. The deep snow left many shops closed and the few that did open their doors could not expect much custom. Even a relatively short walk from the Whitesands to English Street could take anything up to twenty-five minutes as each footstep saw pedestrians sink deep into the snow. In those energy-sapping conditions only those who absolutely had to venture out did so. The absence of traffic made for an unusual, and not unpleasant, silence about the town as people gradually got to grips with the problems. And, in the face of adversity, a spirit of community was born.

People stopped to talk to complete strangers just to discuss the incredible weather and the strange sensation of being cut off from the rest of the world. By late on Tuesday and into the Wednesday morning the first paths had been cleared along pavements and soon after the roads network started to edge nervously back into life as people tackled the enormous drifts that had engulfed many vehicles. By the end of the week an air of normality had returned but the town knew it had been through something special. Many preferred to travel by foot as conditions remained treacherous. Thankfully, the snows did not return but the cost had now to be assessed. Another worry was that floods might follow the snow. Emergency services were put on standby once again and there were concerns that the Nith at the Whitesands could see the worst flooding in its history. While pedestrians were even being warned about the dangers of snow falling from rooftops as the thaw took hold.

Support for the clean-up operation came from the army as around thirty soldiers arrived in town as back-up after the state of emergency was declared over. The men of the Argyll and Sutherland

Highlanders regiment brought six vehicles with them and focussed their efforts on the most remote areas. They helped out local hospitals and ferried helpers to the elderly and other vulnerable people.

One notable military operation involved the delivery of a baby in Kirkbean. Sergeant Gordon McLelland and corporal Steven Rafferty of the Lowland Volunteers battled through the snows along a remote track in an army ambulance to get to the stranded mum-to-be. Luckily they picked up the family doctor along the way and the baby boy was eventually delivered – with the help of paramedics – in the back of the ambulance near New Abbey. A delicate journey followed, including a skid across the icy road, but mother and child were brought safely to Cresswell maternity hospital where they expressed eternal gratitude to the soldiers.

There were also promises of help from politicians as Scottish Office minister Lord Lindsay pledged financial assistance to the region. He visited the council's emergency headquarters and vowed there would be cash available to cover any exceptional costs incurred by the state of emergency. Needless to say, there was a subsequent disagreement about the level of the compensation.

The floods that many thought would follow the snows did not materialise as the thaw proved to be gentler than anticipated. There were concerns that the Nith would pour into the Whitesands and beyond; but these were unfounded, as the weather used a softer hand on Doonhamers than on previous days. By the following week all that was left as a reminder of the phenomenal snow was a few trails of hard-packed ice on some little-used pavements.

Anyone who experienced the winter of 1996 will testify that it was one of the strangest in the history of Dumfries from the moment the snow started to fall. It was amazing how quickly the town switched into emergency mode and how people went to such great lengths to help friends, neighbours and complete strangers. Once the blizzards had been cleared the natural reserve of Doonhamers returned.

Of course, there was a heavy price tag. It took days for the town to get back to normal and many weeks, and in some cases months, before the troubles caused by the freak weather could be repaired. One estimate put the total cost of insurance claims for the period – barely a single day of snow – at anything up to £5 million.

Two businesses in College Street – Huntly's garage and the ATS Tyre depot – were pulled down due to the damage caused by the snow. Huge glass-houses were shattered at garden nurseries when they could not cope with the weight of the snowfall. Dozens of farms reported losing outbuildings or lambing sheds and many domestic properties saw damage to garages and car ports in particular. A spokesman for the local housing authority estimated that damage to its properties – from the likes of roofing and guttering – would be around £50,000.

One of the biggest headaches for the council was that it had to spend money on emergencies and hope to reclaim the money at a later date. The worst snowfalls in fifty years required drastic measures but there was only a limited budget available to pay for them. The council estimated its costs at between £500,000 and £750,000. A spokesman for the council said that it had spent much more than it held in its emergency fund and would now have to look to central government.

The fight for compensation was one that took place at many levels as organisations, businesses and individuals came to terms with the impact of the weather. As time passed most of the financial problems melted away leaving only the memories of an incredible white 'siege' that had afflicted Dumfries for a few days in February. Doonhamers are used to wind and rain but snow is not a meteorological occurrence they have much experience of. That is what made the events of February 1996 so remarkable to a town with a relatively mild climate. Anyone who witnessed the snow now knows that even Dumfries can be hit by freak weather – and also that the town will rally in a crisis.

17

DISASTER STRIKES

No matter how well you think you know your home town it will always have a few surprises in store. One of the attractions of Dumfries for many residents is the relatively quiet life it allows, free from major upset and disaster. But every so often something comes along that shatters the daily routine with its ferocity.

There was no greater disaster at the start of the century than the sinking of the *Titanic* – the supposedly unsinkable White Star liner – in April 1912. The tragedy, although it happened thousands of miles away, struck close to home for Dumfries. Two locals were among the hundreds who lost their lives and their stories were intriguing; and both had very unusual postscripts.

John 'Jock' Hume, of George Street, was a musician with one of the orchestras on board. Reports came through that his ensemble had been playing 'Nearer, my God, to Thee' as the *Titanic* sank. While Thomas Mullin, of Observatory Terrace in Maxwelltown, was a third-class steward who had been well known in local athletics' circles before heading off to sea a few months earlier. Both men, former pupils of St Michael's school, were in their early twenties when they met their death.

Over a year after the disaster a memorial was unveiled in the Dock Park to mark the loss of the two locals. On a beautiful early summer day a large crowd – including members of both families – gathered to see provost Thomson perform the unveiling. He called upon those assembled to give a moment's thought to how the two men had met their deaths. 'Let them fancy what the circumstances would be with the knowledge that they were never to see their school companions again, never to run by the banks of the Nith, never to shake hands with those whom they knew so well; their young lives cut off at once by this dreadful calamity.' As the monument was revealed two buglers played the 'Last Post'. The whole ceremony was brought to a close by the national anthem and the bells of the Midsteeple were sounded.

But this was not the final chapter in the story. Barely a year later reports emerged that Jock Hume's sister, Grace, had been tortured and killed in Belgium by German soldiers shortly after the outbreak of the First World War. The horrific story was carried in both national and local newspapers and was deemed to be further justification for the declaration of war. However, shortly after publication, the story took an unlikely twist when Grace's father received a telegram from his daughter saying simply: 'Reports untrue. Safe in Huddersfield.'

It emerged in a court case in 1914 that letters recounting Grace Hume's alleged demise had been written by her sister Kate, who was charged with 'fabricating and forging' the correspondence. Medical experts were called in to explain why she would have made the story up. One explanation offered was that it was a case of 'adolescent hysteria': she simply convinced herself that what she imagined to have happened was true. And it seems to have found favour with the jury, which took only fifteen minutes to reach its verdict. The foreman announced: 'My lord, we the jury unanimously find the accused guilty of writing the letters as charged, but at the time she did not realise she was committing a crime. We earnestly recommend her to the leniency of the court.'

And, in an unusual step, the Lord Justice General granted the request. He said: 'I am very willing to accede to the earnest recommendation of the jury. They have given most careful attention to your case, and in consideration of the fact that you have already been upwards of three months in prison, having regard to your previous good character, and your youth, I consider it expedient – and this is the order of the court – that you be released now.' Miss Hume burst into tears on hearing she was to be released and this most unusual twist to the *Titanic* tragedy was over.

The tale of Thomas Mullin was to grab newspaper headlines again ninety years after his death. A small, seemingly undistinguished, lot of *Titanic* memorabilia was sold in Dumfries for just over £100 to a Castle Douglas man. It included a pocket watch, steward's badge, postcard and a leather notepad. Little could the purchaser have suspected that the value of the items was substantially higher. Indeed, at a specialist auction in Southampton in 2004, close to £30,000 was raised by a partial sale of the lot. The lucky vendor is still searching for the person who received such a derisory sum in the Dumfries sale. The intention is to ensure that the original seller – believed to be a relative of Mullin – does not miss out on the real value of the memorabilia.

Thankfully disaster has struck only rarely in Dumfries itself but its most regular manifestation has surely been the flooding of the Whitesands and beyond. Heavy rain regularly swells the river Nith and shopkeepers have grown tired of dragging out the sandbags to try to protect their premises. A year rarely goes by when there is not some call for a flood-prevention scheme to minimise the impact of water bursting over the river banks. Many attempts have been made to improve the flood-warning system although this in itself does not prevent water damage.

Some years, of course, are worse than others. In October 1906 some of the most dramatic scenes were witnessed as the Nith overflowed the Whitesands stopping only a short distance from the Hoddam Castle inn. It was reported that a doctor visiting a patient was shocked to find himself up to his waist in water when he tried to leave the premises. While a lorry-man, who had driven his horse into the water, saw the animal almost drown when it slipped and fell. 'The Nithside and Maryholm meadows were one great sheet of water' it was reported.

Every Doonhamer knows that these lessons were never really learned and that there has been little done to deal with the problem. A particularly harsh reminder came at the end of October 1977, when a deluge left parts of the town knee-deep in water – or worse. The bill for the damage caused was estimated at around £250,000. The Kostwise store on the Whitesands reported that it had to replace almost its entire stock as water levels reached five feet; the owners reckoned that about £25,000-worth of stock was ruined and this figure did not include lost custom. Even harder hit was Blacklock and Farries bookshop, for which the estimate of stock ruined was put at £80,000. Others reporting high losses included NR Superstore in Friars Vennel, Barbours in Buccleuch Street and Houston and Wilson's furniture shop. Once again there were claims that traders had not been warned in time and that an up-to-date list of emergency telephone numbers was required. The rapidly expanding housing scheme in Georgetown was also affected by the rains as homeowners in Gilloch Crescent had to be evacuated from their houses.

'It is a long time since such flooding has been seen in Dumfries and by the law of averages most or all of us will be dead before it is seen again' commented the *Dumfries and Galloway Standard* in its editorial. 'This does not mean, however, that the ever-present risk to properties in areas like the Whitesands should be ignored.'

Yet less than five years later, in January 1982, there was a disastrous start to the year as water again swept up Bank Street and into Friars Vennel. By midnight on 3 January the Whitesands was under three feet of water. A slight consolation was that the early-warning system functioned a little better and most traders were able to move stock before the waters reached their highest point. A regional council spokesman at the time reckoned that the lessons from the flood of 1977 had been learned.

And yet there is still a constant threat of flooding in 2005 with heavy downpours likely to close the car parks on the Whitesands. In the worst situations sandbags are deployed but a number of new warning methods have been introduced that should alleviate the problems in the future. If prevention is not an option then at least an early indication of problems to come would be welcome.

While natural phenomena can be a danger, so too are man-made hazards and fire is often the most devastating. A wartime blaze destroyed the junior department of Noblehill school in September 1944. Two passing Sea Scouts spotted the fire at 9.45 p.m. and dashed to tell the headmaster, Mr Welsh, who lived next to his school. The fire brigade were called and arrived within five minutes, only to be greeted by flames licking up through the school roof. Fortunately they were able to confine the damage to the building that housed the junior department and keep the adjoining infant and senior departments largely safe. But the entire contents of the junior school were destroyed. Beds and bedding, cooking utensils and food belonging to the Emergency Relief Organisation were lost. Many library books were destroyed while the school bell still stood in position despite the fact that only the charred remains of the bell tower were still in place. The school was closed for a week to allow pupils from three burnt-out classrooms to be accommodated in other parts of the building. The cause of the blaze was not discovered but it was believed to have started at the rear of the department.

If the swift action of the fire brigade helped keep parts of Noblehill school intact the same could not be said on the night of possibly the most damaging fire in the recent history of Dumfries. Late on Wednesday 10 May 1961, the Roman Catholic St Andrew's cathedral in Brooke Street was completely destroyed by a blaze that probably started in the balcony area. It rapidly spread to the rest of the cathedral leaving just a blackened shell of sandstone where once a proud building had stood. The cathedral – an imposing sandstone structure – dated back to the early nineteenth century and had many fine architectural features, including magnificent stained-glass windows and one of the largest organs in Scotland.

Shortly after eleven, Ian Douglas, of nearby McLellan Street, spotted flames in one of the cathedral windows. He dashed to tell the priest what was happening and the four Sisters of Charity living in the adjoining building were quickly evacuated. A large crowd of spectators was shepherded back to relative safety in English Street as twenty-three fire-fighters fought to bring the blaze under control. One of the most dramatic moments of the night came when the whole roof caved in destroying almost everything underneath. Firemen were forced to retreat and turned their attentions to the belfry, which remains standing to this day on the Shakespeare Street-side of the cathedral. Thankfully, many of the sacred items in the building were saved as they were located in an area that was relatively unaffected by the fire. An emergency renovation fund was launched, which later saw St Andrew's church rise on the same site.

While the school and church fires occurred when both buildings were empty the same could not be said of another fire over a decade later. In November 1977 around four hundred people, including fifty guests, had to be evacuated from the County hotel in High Street after fire broke out in a basement storeroom.

The drama unfolded at around 9 p.m. on Monday, 7 November when a worker spotted smoke coming from a room used for stationery and cleaning materials. The hotel and neighbouring Golden Bull pub were evacuated as the black smoke started to engulf the building. The fire was contained to the storeroom but smoke damage to the rest of the building was extensive. One unfortunate waitress had to be rescued by firemen from a second-floor window after she was trapped by thick smoke. Proprietor Dan Maclachlan later said that the cause of the fire was unclear and added that experts had been called in to investigate. The fifty guests were moved on to other hotels in the town and a planned hairdressing show in the hotel was cancelled.

Dumfries and Galloway Royal Infirmary has to deal with both natural and man-made disasters and over the years has accumulated a lot of experience in this area. The best-known incident was on 21 December 1988 when a Boeing 747 en route to New York – Pan Am flight 103 – was blown up over Lockerbie. No less than 259 passengers and crew and 11 Lockerbie residents were killed that night. But while medical staff braced themselves for a huge influx of casualties, the tide of injured never materialised. Such was the force of the plane crash that there were no survivors. In fact the explosion was so powerful that four million pieces of wreckage were spread over 845 square miles of southern Scotland and northern England.

But the hospital did have to deal with another major accident just a few days after it opened its doors in 1975. Dumfries and Galloway can lay claim to the worst air disaster on Scottish soil (at Lockerbie), the worst Scots rail disaster (at Quintinshill near Gretna where over two hundred died in 1915) and what was, at the time, the worst road accident in Scottish history on the A74 just north of Moffat. That coach crash on Monday 16 June 1975 tested the newly built hospital's capabilities to the full. Six people were killed at the scene of the accident but four lost their lives in the infirmary soon afterwards. Many more were rushed to the new hospital, which ironically was officially opened by the Queen just a few days later.

The accident involved a coach-load of English tourists from Brighton who were heading to the north of Scotland. First reports indicated that a lorry travelling south had burst a tyre and crossed the central reservation before colliding with the coach. One side of the coach was ripped off and it was crushed against a crash barrier. The *Daily Express* vividly described the horror of the aftermath:

> Some of the injured had multiple fractures, others severe head injuries and many had bad spinal injuries and could not move. The seriously injured were gently carried across the road and

> placed in a line on the central reservation. . . . As soon as the first emergency call was received a huge rescue operation swung into action. Doctors, surgeons, and nurses from Dumfries, Beattock and Moffat rushed to the scene as did ambulances from every available spot within twenty miles. At Dumfries, operating theatres were prepared and teams of accident specialists waited for the injured.

In the end the death toll from the crash reached ten. Such was the sterling work done by staff in the new Dumfries hospital that the mayor of Brighton, William Clarke, was moved to make the following statement as the last injured patient left the hospital: 'I wish to pay the sincerest tribute to everyone who has helped and is helping; to the emergency services and the staffs of the Royal Infirmary, Dumfries, and the Law hospital, Carluke, who have all lived up to their highest traditions; and not least to those members of the public who assisted at the scene afterwards.' It was perhaps even more impressive that staff performed so well in what was a new building.

Dumfries has had to cope with its share of disaster over the years, so much so that its emergency planning has become a model that many have imitated. Fire, flood and other calamities have been visited upon the town. As always, they are tackled in the hope that Doonhamers will never have to deal with such situations again – but with the knowledge that fate is unlikely to be that kind.

18

THE NAME GAME

There is a lot that can be learnt about a town simply by walking through it. The worst thing you can do is to keep your head down, ignore the buildings and streets and miss all the stories they have to tell. A simple sign at the corner of a road can impart precious knowledge about recent, and more distant, history. Street names are one of the most obvious, yet most often ignored, sources of information. Sometimes they pick up on the geographical features of an area but in other cases the reason for the name is less obvious. Famous figures from a town's history – perhaps long forgotten – are immortalised, great achievements are commemorated and town councillors are rewarded for years of municipal service.

The procedure in the modern era involves developers suggesting names that may or may not be accepted by local residents and councillors. Sometimes they come back with counter-suggestions, which go back to the local area committee for consideration. Usually these are agreed and this process has seen a number of interesting additions to the history of Dumfries. For example, in 2004, there were more than two hundred houses built at Barnhill and they were named after local places of interest. Hence the names Clunie, Caulstran, Collochan and, most colourfully, Tipperwuppy, entered into the Dumfries street-name directory.

When houses were being built at College Street in the town in 2003 it seemed only natural that the new name should mark one of the town's longest running businesses – Shortridge's laundry –

and Shortridge Court was born. Similarly, a new development at the junction of Queen Street and Shakespeare Street was named to mark the twinning agreement between the town and Gifhorn in Germany; so Gifhorn House was agreed.

One of the most creative pieces of street naming came in 2002 when Queen of the South had just gained promotion from the Scottish second division after many years in the doldrums. The councillor for Ryedale, Tom McAughtrie, ignored the suggested names from the developer for fifty-two new houses in his area: Robison Homes had proposed Minerva Terrace, Minerva Gardens and Minerva Court. Instead, the councillor suggested Bradford Gardens in recognition of Queen of the South chairman Ronnie Bradford, and John Connolly Court as a tribute to the club's promotion-winning manager. In addition, he asked for Stevenson Terrace to mark the name of one of the first families ever to live in Troqueer. Because of the feel-good factor surrounding the football club – which was enjoying bumper crowds at the time – the names suggested by Mr McAughtrie were all agreed.

It was not the only time he had marked sporting achievement in his ward. When Crowther Homes proposed names for its development at Ryedale nurseries, the company had clearly underestimated the degree of imagination required. The names Ryedale, Troqueer and Rossdale were ditched for Houliston Avenue: in tribute to Billy Houliston – who played football for Queens and Scotland – and his brother Max Houliston, the well-known local accordionist. Two other prominent locals were recognised in the naming of Beck Street: former councillor Douglas Beck and his brother Vince, who was active in Troqueer. Finally, Smith Place was put on the map to mark the work of Mary Smith at the local community centre.

One interesting recent tale of street naming came when Senator Homes was building at Barnhill and appeared to have reached agreement on the names Barnhill Court, Barnhill Place and Barnhill Road. However, the company changed its mind and proposed

Turnberry Court, Muirfield Place and Gleneagles Road instead (with clear references to famous golf courses). In council papers from 2002 the reason cited for the change was the developer's concern that there could be difficulties for the emergency services in identifying properties as had occurred at another of their developments. However, after the emergency services were consulted – and raised no objections to the original names – the area committee stuck to the original proposal and Barnhill Road, Court and Place got the nod.

The new method of street naming may be most democratic with its council consultation but, in truth, it follows criteria that have been in existence for centuries. As a rule, the geographic location of a street is a big factor, as is the person most involved with its construction while commemorating the famous is another common practice. These threads can be seen in modern street names but they were also prevalent when the process of naming vennels, alleys and paths began.

Some of the oldest names are among the most obvious so the likes of Irish Street, English Street, Moffat Road, Edinburgh Road, Lockerbie Road, Dalbeattie Road, Castle Douglas Road, New Abbey Road and Annan Road simply indicate the direction in which roads travelled. While others got their names from buildings or landmarks. That explains the likes of Shakespeare Street (home of the Theatre Royal), Academy Street (Dumfries Academy), Nith Place (river Nith), St Michael Street (with the eponymous church), Friars Vennel (the old Greyfriars church), Castle Street (the former castle of the Maxwell family) or Loreburn Street (for the burn that flowed alongside it).

Similarly straightforward explanations suffice for the likes of Bank Street (where many banks found a home in the nineteenth century), Assembly Street (it housed the old assembly rooms), Pumpfield Lane (which led to a well), Barnslaps (a gap between barns), Brewery Street (obviously a home for brewing), College

Street (led to the College of Lincluden), Mill Road (led to a watermill at the Caul on the Nith) and Mill Brae (which led to the old windmill that is now Dumfries museum). While the extinct volcano of Criffel gives its name to a number of streets: Avenue, Court, Road and Drive. And the names the Stoop and Stoop Loaning come from the turning point on the Lockerbie Road where horse racing took place. Glebe Street is so named because it occupies land that belonged to St Michael's church; glebe means land granted to a clergyman as part of his income. And Lovers Walk was for hundreds of years a country lane, hence its romantic name. Less obvious might be the Corbelly and Corberry names, which feature on a number of street names. It is said they derive from the Gaelic *corbaile*, which means a settlement on a round hill and given their location in the town around the convent hill, this seems a reasonable explanation.

One of the most intriguing names is Bane Loaning which leads up to Dumfries High School. Apparently this was where bones were discovered from the mass graves dug to cope with the after-effects of the plague. At one point the street would have been outside the town boundary making the name a slightly gruesome reminder of the area's past.

Of course, the great and good have provided more than their share of names starting of course with Queen Street (for Queen Victoria) and Great King Street (for George V). There is also a regal feel to the likes of George Street and Charlotte Street, in honour of George III and his queen. Victoria Avenue and Road and Albert Road commemorate Queen Victoria and her husband Albert, the prince consort. Then there are Elizabeth Walk (for the present Queen) and Margaret Walk (for her sister, the late Princess Margaret). Local nobility also get its dues in the form of Buccleuch Street, for the Duke of Buccleuch, a major local landowner; Queensberry Street and Square are named after the third Duke of Queensberry. Devorgilla Bridge and Terrace remember Lady Devorgilla, the owner of much of Galloway in the Middle Ages; Balliol Avenue was called after her son John Balliol, King of Scotland from 1292 until he was stripped of the royal insignia in 1296, earning him the name of *Toom Tabard* (literally, empty surcoat). Fergus, the first Lord of Galloway – born around 1078 – is recognised by Fergus Avenue.

Other famous figures with connections to local streets include: the Maxwell family (Maxwell Street); the Lauries of Maxwelltown (Laurieknowe); the Hood family, which owned nurseries in the area (Hood's Loaning); the Maxwell family of Munches (Munches Street).

Individuals, too, have found their good works marked for posterity. Brooms Road, for example, commemorates James Broom a Dumfries town clerk of the nineteenth century. Other council officers or local politicians to have found similar fame include: town clerks John and R. A. Grierson (Grierson Avenue); their fellow town clerk William Martin (Martin Avenue); MP William Ewart, who fought for free libraries and museums, is twice remembered at both the Ewart Library and Ewart Walk. Born in Liverpool, Ewart was elected for a number of constituencies in England before representing Dumfries in 1841. He helped to draft the Public Libraries Act, which became law in 1850.

Others to find recognition were councillor Mrs Charteries whose family part-owned a number of mills in the area (Charteries Avenue), Maxwelltown town council's bailie Hill (Hill Avenue), joint town clerk Alexander Sharpe (Sharpe Crescent), councillor Alexander Steel (Steel Avenue), Maxwelltown provost Philip Forsyth (Forsyth Street), provost David Brodie (Brodie Avenue) and provost Ernie Robertson (Robertson Avenue). Primrose Street and Gordon Street were named after partners in the local solicitors' firm one of whom, James Gordon, was also provost in the 1860s. Former burgh surveyor Robert Osborne is recalled by Osborne Crescent and Drive. While Nelson Street carries the name of Esther Nelson, the mother of the well-known businessman and provost John Chicken, who wisely avoided the use of his surname. Aldermanhill Road recognises the use of alderman as an alternative word for provost. And, of course, there is Gladstone Road, which bears the name of William Ewart Gladstone – the original Grand Old Man of British politics – who was prime minister four times in the late nineteenth century.

Arts and entertainment get more than their share of credit among the street names of the town. J. M. Barrie – whose character Peter Pan was inspired by the author's early life in Dumfries – has Barrie Avenue. Brooke Street is thought to recognise the nineteenth-century actor Gustavus Brooke, who drowned on his way to Australia in 1866 but had performed in Dumfries earlier in his career while Darlison Avenue was named in recognition of drama producer John Darlison. The various Aird's – which include Avenue, Drive and Court – are a tribute to Thomas Aird, the poet, and a former editor of the *Dumfries and Galloway Courier and Herald*. Born in Roxburghshire, he published several volumes of verse – which received favourable reviews from the likes of Thomas Carlyle – before his death in Dumfries in 1876. Local writer and librarian George Shirley, the originator of Guid Nychburris, has his work appreciated by Shirley Road. And Hugh MacDiarmid, a native of Langholm in Dumfries and Galloway, finds a home in Heathhall's MacDiarmid Road.

Robert Burns, of course, has a fitting tribute with Burns Street but there are also numerous mentions of his work, friends and acquaintances in the streets around Dumfries and Galloway golf course. The likes of Armour Drive (after wife Jean), Ellisland Drive (where he lived), Alloway Road (where he was born), Oliphant Court (where he farmed) or Syme Road (after friend John Syme) are just a handful of examples. Other streets that can cite a Burns connection include Gilbert Circle (his brother's name), Afton Drive (mentioned in song) and Dalswinton Avenue (home of his landlord). Only Sir Walter Scott can challenge the Bard with Waverley Road, Peveril Court, Ashton Drive, Deans Road and Kenilworth Road all taking their names from his work.

Religious figures have not been overlooked. Irving Street was named after Annan-born Edward Irving, a controversial preacher who was convicted of heresy in 1833 and later developed the Irvingite Church. Wallace Street takes the name of the former minister of St Michael's, the Revd Robert Wallace, while Babbington – recognised in a number of names – is reckoned to be a misspelling of the Episcopalian minister of Dumfries, the Revd William Babington. There is a religious feel to the name of Troqueer Road too, since it is derived from the farmstead of St Queran. St Queran was a ninth century saint and St Queran's well – believed to have healing properties – was situated on the outskirts of the town.

Those people responsible for building streets, or donating land, are also remembered. Hence, Adam Newall – who was married to Catherine Rae – built three streets in the 1800s which carry their names: Newall Terrace, Rae Street and Catherine Street. Goldie Avenue gets its name from Jean Goldie, who left money to buy a public park for the people of Maxwelltown. While the gifting of land saw James Gordon Hamilton-Starke recognised with Hamilton Avenue and Starke Crescent in Troqueer. Kirkowens Street marks the name of builder Thomas Kirk and his wife Agnes Owens. While James Avenue is reputed to have taken the name of James Murray who built a house off Terregles Street and, when others were added, the street took his name. Similarly Dempster Place carries the name of the grocer who built the houses in order to provide homes for families who would be affected by the sale of his shop to Woolworth. Scots-American Andrew Carnegie saw his generosity in donating £10,000 towards the Ewart Library enough to earn him Carnegie Street. More recently, builders like R. K. Brown recognised his wife's maiden name in Richmond Avenue. Fellow builders Robison and Davidson are linked to Robert's Crescent and Robison Drive (after Robert Robison the founder), Averill Crescent (wife of Robert Robison) and Grant's Court after a former managing director of the firm.

There are nods to great historical events in the name of Union Street, which marks the amalgamation of Dumfries and Maxwelltown. While Verdun Place was completed during the First World War and named after the battle being fought at the time the work was carried out. And Wallace's Loaning is thought to mark the visit paid by William Wallace to the town in 1297. Minden Drive, Crescent and Avenue were named to mark one of the battle honours of local regiment, the King's Own Scottish Borderers. The battle of Minden in 1759 – against the French – was one of the first won by infantry attacking cavalry and the regiment still marks Minden Day on 1 August. Intriguingly, Jock's Loaning is believed to be named after a local character from the area who chased away courting couples with a stick.

With the council having earmarked land between the Moffat Road and Edinburgh Road in 2004 for several hundred new houses – and demand for property still soaring – there are likely to be many new street names added to the Dumfries landscape in the future. And they will all tell their own little story about the history of the town in the twenty-first century and beyond.

19

SHOPS AND CHANGES

There are few places where the face of a town changes more than in its main shopping streets. The passing of time sees some stores fade from popularity while others go from strength to strength. Whole trades disappear to be replaced by new ones while other shops adapt to survive in the changed economic environment. The rise in disposable income and the move towards supermarkets and chain stores have transformed towns and villages across Great Britain. Dumfries has not been immune to this with some famous store names being lost, bought over or transformed. It is fascinating to see how the demands of the shopping public – and how they were catered for – have changed.

The priorities in Dumfries at the end of the nineteenth century must have been very different from today judging by some of the prominent businesses that featured in Stratten's *Guide to Glasgow and its Environs*. For clothing, one would look no further than Andrew Patterson, at 62 High Street, near the fountain, which enjoyed a 'numerous and influential clientele . . . which embraces the elite of the resident nobility and gentry in Dumfries and its environments.' Little wonder he catered for the upper end of the market since among the clothes stocked were shooting and yachting suits entirely 'bespoke' and provided by a staff of twelve.

More down-to-earth attire was provided by Douglas Wylie, at his store in the Plainstones. This shop sold waterproof coats, capes, leggings and oilskin goods. Other big names in the trade as Dumfries moved towards the 1900s were MacGowan and Co (drapers, silk mercers, clothiers, hatters and shirtmakers) and Robert Barbour (silk mercer, clothier, ladies' and gentlemen's outfitter) both of which occupied High Street sites. Of MacGowan's, Stratten's *Guide* comments: 'In the important making-up sections they enjoy the support of the fashionable residents of the town and district, both ladies and gentlemen, and their capabilities go without saying.' While Barbour's: 'Enjoys, we need not say, a high-class and representative patronage, and fully merits the reputation he has won by the skilful and accomplished way in which he has so long directed the operations of his fashionable department.'

The rural and agricultural nature of the town was seen in other businesses of note in 1891 Dumfries, including J. T. Aitchison's impressive Central Fish, Game and Poultry Mart at the Greyfriars Church end of the High Street with a double frontage onto Church Place and Castle Street. Another prominent business was Messrs Fotheringham and Company, which operated from the old corn exchange but which, by then, sold seeds of all types. In fact there was an impressive variety of shops: John Chicken of Maxwelltown offered 'fancy bread and biscuits'; A Thomson the ironmonger of Queensberry Street could furnish 'one of the largest and most varied stocks . . . tastefully arranged'; John Sutherland's High Street chemist provided 'his well-known Nerolyne Cream of Roses, for rendering the skin beautifully soft, smooth and white'; and Robert Armstrong and Sons tea, wine and coffee merchants – as well as aerated water manufacturers – boasted sites in English Street and Assembly Street that purveyed 'aerated beverages of all kinds, such as lemonade, soda water, kali water, seltzer, sarsaparilla and the like'.

Times change, and by the 1930s a stroll along the High Street provided a different view although some of the big names from past decades were still in business. Down one side of the High Street local shoppers could find the likes of Shortridge and Sons, Fusco's

Café and Soda Fountain Bar, the Lyceum Theatre, the Co-op, MacGowan and Co, Robinson Bros, *The Courier and Herald* newspaper offices, Home and Colonial Stores, Woolworths, Greenlees and Sons, Easiphit Footwear and G. Young and Son. While on the 'even' side of High Street were J. J. Scott Ltd, the Magneto Accumulator and Electro Plating Company, Co-op Insurance, Cooper and Co with their 'celebrated teas', the Dundee Equitable Boot Depot and Andrew Rankine, ironmongers.

If it was a 'famed hot pie' you were after in 1932 then the only place to go was Thomson Bros bakers, which had stores in Queen Street, English Street and Queensberry Street. While the dubious pleasure of Chilprufe pure wool underwear could be purchased from M. J. McGeorge in Castle Street. There was 'artistic painting and decorating' on offer from William Haining and Sons in Friars Vennel. And James Dickson and Son, plumbers of Buccleuch Street, promised that 'jobbing work will receive prompt and personal attention and be executed by reliable plumbers'.

Those in search of furniture would have been easily persuaded by the adverts for Johnstone and Brown's High Street store, which reckoned it was 'the house for artistic carpets and soft furnishings in reliable quantities at keen prices'. If, on the other hand, your eyesight was of concern you could 'see with the eyes of your youth' by visiting Thos G. Park Optician just a few doors away. Other health needs could be catered for at Alexander Turner chemist in Buccleuch Street, which sold 'Turner's Tonic Elixir – a splendid pick me up'. A relatively new addition to the scene was the general post office in Great King Street, constructed in 1926.

Tearooms dominated the eating options of the time with the Central and Steeple tearooms on the High Street and the Ship dining rooms on Whitesands. Other options were the Imperial restaurant in Queensberry Square and the Royal restaurant at Burns Statue. Among the hotels of the day were the County, King's Arms, New George and Globe – all in the High Street – and the Eden Temperance hotel in English Street, the White Hart and Royal Oak in Brewery Street and the Salutation hotel in Market Square.

A number of these names will be familiar to modern readers as some of them had survived as pubs into the twenty-first century. Among the 'spirit dealers and wine merchants' of 1932 that still had a spot in the town more than seventy years later were the Coach and Horses, Dickie's, the Liver Inn, the Globe Inn at Market Square, Railway Inn, Victoria Inn, the Fleshers, the Ship Inn and the Hole I' th' Wa'. Names that have disappeared include the Golden Bull on the High Street, Maxwell Arms in Irish Street, the Forrester's Arms in Queensberry Street, the Queen's Arms on the High Street, the Wool Pack Inn on Loreburn Street, the Rob Roy Inn on Queensberry Street, the Hoddam Castle on Whitesands, the Marshall Arms in English Street and Dumfries Arms on Whitesands.

About a decade further on, in 1941, further changes had taken place in a town now at war. Among the cosmetic changes to Dumfries was the 1938 opening in the Dock Park of the R. A. Grierson Rest and Recreation Room as a tribute to a man who had been town clerk for thirty-one years. While the following year the government started work on an RAF aerodrome on the 300-acre farm at Tinwald Downs.

Despite the war Doonhamers should have been having a wonderful time if the adverts of the day were anything to go by. The impressive Imperial reckoned itself to be 'the finest restaurant in Scotland' while the Regal called itself 'the Queen of Cinemas'. And the owners of the Nithside restaurant on the Whitesands believed that no visit to Dumfries was complete without going through its doors. New hotels in the *Post Office Directory for Dumfries, Maxwelltown and District* were the Cairndale on English Street and the Queensberry, which was on the same road but closer to the town centre. Restaurants mentioned for the first time in the *Directory* were Setti's Regal café in English Street, the CR café in the High Street ('any special dish made to order – only the very best quality food served') and Fusco's in Friars Vennel. The Plaza on the High Street offered dancing on Monday, Wednesday and Saturday and proudly rated itself as the ideal venue for 'whist drives and coming of age parties'.

On the High Street during the Second World War you could find Nethertown Dairies, which was happy to sell 'produce of over 200 tuberculin-tested cows from our own farms'. While Pearson's had made quite an impact in Friars Vennel with three separate stores – at numbers 77, 80 and 84 – specialising in clothes for babies, ladies, gents and in sportswear. And if your interest was 'model railways, the most fascinating hobby in the world' there was nowhere better to visit than George D. Campbell on the High Street. For more active pursuits there was Young's Sports Emporium, which was one of the biggest draws in the town at the time.

One of the most significant stores on the scene was now Binns department store at 89 High Street, which opened in 1933. Its catchphrase was 'shop at Binns for everything' and it was proud to advertise an electric lift to its café where the discerning shopper could find 'everything that goes to make a real cosy and comfortable restaurant'. The store was a Dumfries institution for several decades, before it closed and was replaced by the Bank of Scotland.

Also on the High Street at the time were Dinwiddie Printers with a 'large staff of men of long experience each a specialist in his own job', the Fifty Shilling Tailors who won no prizes for the originality of their name and MacGowan and Co at the Plainstones, which reckoned that if 'you want the best possible value – we give it'. While Barbours in Buccleuch Street was putting the emphasis on quality with the motto: 'Ladies and gentlemen whose good taste demands clothing not only of the highest quality but of the most up to date style invariably visit Barbours'.

Meanwhile, bedding and slip covers were a speciality for Gordon M. N. Pattie in Queensberry Street, Percy Bros offered radio expertise in English Street and Esse cookers were all the rage at Robert Armstrong and Sons in Church Crescent. And H. Spence Culbert the chemist vowed: 'If you must take medicine, why not make sure you take the best and purest obtainable'.

By the 1950s there was a discernible boom in fields like entertainment (both at home and outside), eating out and domestic appliances. The opening of Gracefield Arts Centre in 1951 was one demonstration of how demand was changing. Also finding a spot in the town was Gardiner and Ball at the corner of Buccleuch Street and Whitesands, which specialised in radios and televisions – as did Grierson and Graham from a store opposite Dumfries Academy where prams and motorcycles were also on offer.

Goods once considered a luxury were now within the reach of many and this trend was highlighted by the likes of Sutherland Motors where Humber, Hillman, Sunbeam-Talbot and Commer cars were available. World Travel at Church Crescent promised 'all types of travel arranged to all parts of the world.' While people looking for toys could find them at Newall's in Friars Vennel – which offered among its star attractions the Dumfries Doll's Hospital – or at the Radio Doctor on the Whitesands. And there was hardly a more popular place for a haircut than Joyce's hairdressing salon on the High Street where 'your loveliness is our business'.

Pearson's went from strength to strength, and had now stretched out its presence in the Vennel and also offered carpet and lino from a new Church Crescent base. While Dinwiddies was delighted to quote an English visitor saying that, 'Dumfries district is fortunate in having in its midst such a fine printing and bookbinding plant'. W. J. Kelly on the High Street was proud to be an official Hoover outlet. While a hint at the tastes of the day is given by Matthew Fleming the butcher touting for trade for his 'sausages, corned beef and pickled tongues'.

But the most significant change was in the catering sector, largely fuelled by the influx of Italian immigrants, and among the eateries listed in the 1953 business guide to the town were a whole host of new cafes, dining rooms and fish restaurants. These include the Café Continentale on Great King Street, the Central café (Pioli's) on English Street, the College café in St Michael Street, Glover's dining rooms on the Whitesands, Fusco's in Friars Vennel, the Locarno café on the Whitesands, Marcucci's and Matthews café in the Vennel, the Noblehill Park café, Oughton's, the Palmerston café on Glasgow Street, Pierotti's on the Whitesands, the Regal café, the St Michael's café, Verrachia and Toni as well as the Victory restaurant in the High Street. The great majority of these establishments had some link to Italy as café culture boomed in Dumfries. And pubs, of course, never went out of fashion with names like the Great Eastern Spirit Vaults in English Street, the Haddows Inn in Market Street, the Billy Bar in the High Street, the New Bazaar on the Whitesands, the Queen of the South in Nith Place and the Spread Eagle popping up.

The expansion of the service sector continued into the 1960s and 1970s when the likes of the Bendix Self-Service Launderette promised 'your family wash done automatically while you go shopping in 30 minutes'. At this stage, the town remained the preserve of smaller, independent retailers as witnessed with a quick glance at the names occupying High Street stores in 1960. Walking along the side nearest the Nith you would have passed stores including the New George Hotel, G. J. McDowall outfitters, E. R. Bell's painter and decorators, the Lyceum Theatre, Jean Edwards tobacconist, R. Bouskill & Son bakers, the Queen's Arms, Gunyon & Douglas fishmonger and butcher, the Billy Bar, the County hotel, McGowan & Co drapers, RS McColl confectioners, Binns, W. J. Kelly ironmongers, S. Redmayne tailors, Timpson's shoe shop, Matthew Fleming butchers, Halford Cycle Company, Dumfriesshire Newspapers, Johnstone's blacksmiths, Boots the chemist, Dinwiddies printers and stationers, Graftons fashions, Johnson Brothers dyers, Home & Colonial grocers, Tyler's boots and shoes, the *Dumfries and Galloway Standard*, the Labour Party office, the

Victory restaurant, Maypole Dairy Co, Hosiery Manufacturing Company, Brighter Homes, Edward Ewen jeweller, R. Johnstone & Son grocers, National Bank of Scotland, McDougall Bros commission agents, the Fifty Shilling Tailors, Scotch Wool and Hosiery Stores, Woolworths, Greenlees & Sons shoe shop, Birrell confectioners, the New Plaza Ballroom and restaurant, William Byers fruiterers, the Cigarette Box, J. M. McLean jeweller, J. Turner fishmonger, Johnstone's ladies' and children's outfitters and G. Young and Son sports outfitters. The opposite side boasted, among others, H. Grierson hairdresser, Fruit Bazaar Ltd, The Toy Shop (Newall's), McDougall Bros, Scottish Rapid Cleaners, Joyce hairdressing salon, Drummond plumbers, S & S bakery, Kennedy & Son seedsmen, James Wallace butchers, Margaret Todd fruiterer, the Rainbow restaurant, J. Bogie & Son seedsmen, Brotherston bakers, James Player grocers, the Globe Inn, Scottish Gas Board, James Swan newsagent, John Hall confectioner, the Mitchell private library, W. Muir hairdresser, J & J Scott Ltd, Dumfries Motor Company, the Kings Arms, John Fraser chemist, the *Galloway News*, Millers (butchers), Lipton's grocers, George Graham hairdresser, J. Reid & Co shoe shop, David Colthart drapers, Montague Burton Ltd tailors, James Reid gents outfitters, the Magneto Accumulator and Electro Plating Company and Turner & Co refrigerated sales. At the Midsteeple there was Joseph Shandley confectioners, South-West Area District Electricity Board, R. Kerr tobacconist, G. Currie fruiterer, John McColl butcher and Dumfries & Maxwelltown Co-operative Society before continuing along the High Street with Alexander Gray shoe shop, William Coulthart chemist, James Grant & Co house furnishers, Cooper & Co grocers, Dumfriesshire Liberal Association, Thomas Thomson watch-makers, Oliver & McLean wine merchants, DE Shoe Service, H. M. Payne wool shop, D. Simpson tobacconist, the Hole I' the Wa' Inn, Thomson Bros bakers, Willson's Ltd ladies outfitters, Andrew Rankin ironmonger and Paige ladies outfitters.

Even by 1970 the number of independent retailers was still high. In bookmaking none of the big names operated in the town and the 'turf' was split between the likes of Bertucci and Brown in St Michael Street, D. M. Craik in Glasgow Street, Bill Gallie in English Street, Jacky Law in Queen Street, McDougall and Co in High Street and College Street, John Ratcliffe and Sons on the Whitesands and A. Toni at Noblehill Park. But the times were changing and one of the most significant developments was the decline of the King's Arms at the old South Gate of the town. In 1974 locals were told there was little hope of retaining the building since it posed a significant fire risk and had serious structural defects. And by 1976 the condition of the bottom end of the High Street prompted the *Dumfries and Galloway Standard* to run a front page story with the stark headline, 'A High Street Named Dereliction'. The rest of the town fared little better with visitors said to be appalled by empty buildings like the huge Imperial restaurant, the former Armstrong's ironmongery in Church Crescent, Turner's fish shop in the High Street. In total they counted some thirty-eight premises lying empty.

The turnaround was slow but throughout the 1980s, 1990s and into the new millennium there has been a pronounced trend for chain stores on the High Street. At the same time out-of-town supermarkets all but killed off small grocers, tobacconists and the like in the centre of Dumfries. Big arrivals included Marks and Spencer at the fountain end of the High Street, later to be joined by the sizeable Loreburne shopping centre that also predominantly featured national chains. By 2005 a walk along the now pedestrianised High Street painted a very different picture to the one of forty years ago. The Sony Centre, Marks and Spencer, Ottakar's bookshop, Thornton's chocolates, Vodafone, River Island, WH Smith, Woolworths, H. Samuel, Littlewoods, Greggs the bakers and other national players dominated the scene. There had also been a significant rise in the number of charity shops occupying prominent sites and the phenomenon of the cut-price 'pound-shop' had also made a major impact on both the main thoroughfare and on side streets. And banks and building societies had also taken a keen grip, with the Bank of Scotland, Abbey plc, Alliance and Leicester, Bradford and Bingley, Clydesdale, Royal Bank of Scotland and Cumberland Building Society all boasting High Street premises with the Woolwich and Nationwide just off the main thoroughfare. Indeed, by the start of the twenty-first century locals would have been hard pushed to name the owners of any shop – let alone spot them walking up Friars Vennel – such was the predominance of the chain store. Ladbrokes bookmakers, Clarks, DE and Barratts shoe shops, Nobles Amusements, Bakers Oven, Birthdays Ltd and Game were some of the other names to be found along the High Street frontage.

Out of town, Tesco completed a massive store at Cuckoo Bridge in the second half of 2004, which signalled the continuing trend away from the small retailer. And fellow supermarket giant Lidl was also planning investment on the Brooms Road site opposite the already imposing Safeway store, which was in the process of changing its name to Morrisons. There were still some familiar names but few had a High Street presence. Pattie's outdoor wear still traded from Queensberry Street and Barbours still occupied a large site in Buccleuch Street. Only in the smaller streets could local outfits be found.

And it seemed unlikely at the start of the twenty-first century that things would stand still. Plans were on the table for car-parking charges to be introduced to help fund the regeneration of Dumfries. It was hoped this would allow other ambitious plans to come to fruition. Among the major investment mooted for the town was a leisure complex on the old Co-op site. Ambitious plans for a revamp of the Theatre Royal were also seeking funding. And it was hoped that some sort of cultural centre could be created for the town on two centres – one around the Ewart Library area with the other on the Whitesands.

Whatever happens in the future there has been a dramatic transformation that mirrors other towns in Scotland. Anyone dropped into Dumfries after thirty years away would hardly recognise any of today's stores. Maybe with the demands of the consumer it will always be that way. And it will be truly interesting to watch how the town changes further in the decades to come.

20

TO HELL AND BACK

Travel a few miles along any road out of Dumfries and you will receive a sharp reminder of how big a part the land has played in its history. Agriculture and the town have gone hand in hand since its foundation. In modern times it may have drifted from its roots as a market town but there are still countless links to the countryside.

At least once a year Dumfries is given a reminder in the strongest possible terms of just how dependent it is on farms and farming. The annual Dumfries and Lockerbie Show at Park farm in August is, as tradition would have it, when country comes to town. Nowadays it has taken on the air of a celebration of rural life but it also serves as an important reminder. The town could not exist without the farms around it and the reverse is also true.

The relationship between the two is normally cause for celebration, if sometimes a little antagonism – usually when trapped behind a tractor on Dumfries bypass. But one of the most brutal demonstrations of how crucial agriculture is to the area came at the start of 2001 and it is one that no one will ever forget. Although foot-and-mouth disease did not have a direct effect at the heart of Dumfries it hit almost every aspect of day-to-day life across south-west Scotland. Nobody could have anticipated how dramatic the impact would be of a virulent outbreak of this killer of animal life.

The news broke at the end of February that six farms in the region had been cordoned off amid fears that the disease – which had started in north-east England – had reached Scotland. By far the worst affected area was Annandale and Eskdale with the first farm hit right in the heart of Lockerbie. But the problems stretched across the region and Dumfries itself was to be the nerve centre for the fight back. It was in the Queen of the South that battle plans were drafted and they earned high praise. Other parts of the country recognised their debt to the methodical, detailed and dramatic steps taken in the south-west.

It was a matter of days before the effects of the disease and the government's response were seen – and smelled – across the area. Animals were being valued and slaughtered in increasing numbers and from Lockerbie and Canonbie in the east the disease spread north towards Auldgirth, rapidly surrounding Dumfries. Then the awful pyres were built that led to the most hellish scenes witnessed in modern farming as hundreds of carcasses were burned. Movement restrictions were imposed on farms to reduce the risk of the disease spreading, which added to the feeling of a siege mentality. Buckets of disinfectant appeared everywhere as the public, as well as the farming community, was encouraged to do what it could to stop foot-and-mouth in its tracks. 'We know it is a difficult time' said William McIntyre of the National Farmers Union of Scotland. 'But we have to appeal to people, farmers and the general public, to abide by the rules.'

That the disease was bound to have an effect outside agriculture was quickly felt as any mass gathering was a potential hazard. So, the sporting world effectively shut down to block escape routes for foot-and-mouth. Queen of the South's derby game against Stranraer was postponed. Football matches in the South and East league were cancelled. The South league in particular had a number of teams from rural parts of Dumfries and Galloway with many players either living on farms or having access to them. It was reckoned the risk was too great and the fixtures were cancelled. The president of the South league, Colin Holden, explained: 'With so many of the grounds being surrounded by farmland, we decided we would call off the matches.'

Rugby was also affected and even curling fixtures at Dumfries Ice Bowl were victims of the disease. Understandably, the Dumfriesshire hunt point-to-point, held on farmland near Lockerbie, was a victim while even the Dumfries Running Club felt the effect when its New Millennium marathon – planned for March – was hit. There seemed to be no walk of life that was left untouched. Schools were closed or pupils on farms in the area were forced to stay at home for fear the disease might extend its grip.

As the situation worsened it became clear that local vets were in no position to cope with the number of animals that needed to be examined and then slaughtered. The Army was drafted in to help with the cull, which only added to the feeling that the region was under attack. There was rarely a day that went by in Dumfries, and its surrounding towns and villages, when a military vehicle was not seen patrolling the streets.

In one awful week parents at three primary schools around Dumfries complained that their children had witnessed the cull of animals. Duncow, Caerlaverock and Cargenbridge all had the horror of the situation brought home to them in the starkest way. Much was being done to minimise the impact but at the same time the necessity for swift action did not always make sensitivity the top priority. At Duncow it was claimed a pyre was lit an hour before the end of term, at Cargenbridge a parent said the school hardly had time to close curtains before the cull began on a nearby farm and at Caerlaverock it was reported that pupils left the school to see a lorry loaded with carcasses. The Scottish Executive confirmed that it would be investigating the incidents.

There was hardly a family that was not affected. Everything was masterminded, as it had been during the heavy snows of 1996, through the council 'bunker' (the informal name for the control room set up in English Street to deal with the crisis). It did its best to coordinate the approach to combating the illness that was threatening to destroy so many livelihoods. The financial impact on farms was obvious but the draconian measures put in place to deal with the crisis were also having a big effect on other businesses. Scenes of burning animals devastated tourism while travel restrictions meant that every line of work saw trade turn down significantly. As major political figures visited to see the problems for themselves one of the first things they were asked about was the level of aid that would be offered to help the region back onto its feet.

Henry McLeish, at that time Scotland's first minister, pledged to give maximum support to Dumfries and Galloway and praised the way the fight had been taken to the disease. He commented: 'I think we owe it to Dumfries and Galloway Council to stand four-square with them and by doing so show the community that we are genuinely interested in helping.' There was little doubt by the time of his visit – at the end of March – that the area needed financial help. Not only was the policy of culling infected animals being followed with military zeal but also the controversial contiguous cull – where farms close to infected areas also had their stock killed – was hitting hard.

After the first minister there was a visit from the prime minister, Tony Blair, who faced the media outside council headquarters in English Street, Dumfries. He sent out a personal message to the people of the region after meeting with business leaders and farmers and also saw at first hand the giant burial pit at Birkshaw forest near Lockerbie. After the meeting the prime minister made a statement:

> I was left in no doubt about the dark shadow the disease has cast over this area. But what also struck me was the impressive determination from everyone at this meeting – and this whole community – to work together to overcome this crisis. Even those farmers who spoke of their agony at watching their animals slaughtered back the tough action being taken to contain and eradicate foot-and-mouth here.

At the time Mr Blair was making his speech the number of confirmed outbreaks in the region had risen to over one hundred. The disease was striking outwith the original hotspots in Annandale and Eskdale and now included Kirkbean, Holywood, Shawhead and many other places. The number of sheep culled already totalled over 100,000 while cattle figures had gone over 20,000. There was a cautious belief that the pre-emptive cull was helping to slow down the spread of the disease but there was fear every time a new case sprung up in a new area.

The prime minister promised that £150 million in compensation was available for those whose animals had been slaughtered but a few weeks after his visit there were desperate calls for cash to come on stream more quickly. The council put its extra costs at over £4 million, with another £6.25 million earmarked for an aid package. The impact on small business across the region was hard to measure but an estimate of £100 million was made in the middle of April. The delay in delivering on promises was frustrating many in the region and prompted Langholm councillor Denis Male to comment of the Scottish Executive: 'They are fumbling around without coming clean and committing cash. We have seen our communities ripped apart, half our farms have gone and the public feel that we are not shouting loud enough on their behalf. But we have been asking for answers right from the start.' He summed up feelings of isolation and frustration that were not uncommon at the time.

Meanwhile, the crisis was claiming more high-profile events with the Guid Nychburris celebrations in Dumfries – of which the ride-outs of horses are such an integral part – quickly cancelled. And, understandably, the Dumfries and Lockerbie Show at Park farm was unlikely to go ahead given the enormous loss of stock and the dangers inherent in holding a gathering in an area so deeply hit by the disease.

Eventually, thanks to the dedication of those involved – and not without a lot of suffering – the outbreak was brought under control and slowly restrictions were lifted. Gradually, light appeared at the end of the hellish tunnel that both farming and the wider community had been travelling through. However, foot-and-mouth left significant problems in its wake and measures were introduced to deal with them: a fast-track payment scheme was introduced to help small businesses; and interest-free loans and grants were made available by Scottish Enterprise (Dumfries and Galloway) to help business. While these packages were appreciated there was some criticism that more cash had not been made available.

Farmers, too, were trying to come to terms with what had happened and seeking appropriate compensation. Many high-value bloodlines had been lost and would cost a fortune to replace. While these large compensation packages grabbed the headlines it would be wrong to forget the devastating effects on family farms. Many had not been directly infected but had undergone the pre-emptive cull in an attempt to help their colleagues elsewhere and form a barrier against the disease. For some, it would be the final straw in a business they felt had taken too many hits in recent times. But for others it was time to take a fresh look at how they ran their farms and examine ways of moving on, learning lessons and praying that it would never happen again.

Happier times were around the corner. A region so steeped in agriculture showed an amazing resilience by coming back from a crisis that had wrought havoc. Slowly, as land was brought back into use the laborious process of restocking began and farmers showed that they had not been beaten. In summer 2002, the Dumfries and Lockerbie show returned to the show field at Park farm. It was an event that showed the determination of the community. There is little doubt that there was a sombre element to the proceedings after such dark times and yet there was a clear desire by organisers to look forward rather than dwell upon the past. Secretary Esther Bicket spoke hopefully about the show and the plans for the future:

> We have taken the opportunity to broaden the show's range of activities to appeal to both those who live in rural areas and those from urban areas and we are really building for the future. The show will appeal to a very broad range of people. We are particularly pleased to be able to welcome back the livestock competitions and the agricultural community missing last year because of foot-and-mouth. We are very pleased with the number of entries we have, which are encouraging. Most exhibitors from the past are back again this year but with fewer animals. However, there are new exhibitors too. Obviously, overall, they are down on the Year 2000 but it is a good base to build up for the future.

The weather decided not to show any particular emotion as heavy rains dogged the event but it was back in some style. Not long afterwards, the rural development minister Ross Finnie – so under fire during the crisis – paid tribute to the efforts that had been made to spare the rest of the country. On a visit to the area he said:

> Suffering in this area was particularly harsh and there is a lot of recovery work going on now. When I was at the Scottish sheep show I spoke to people from Dumfries and Galloway who had suffered. I have been watching very closely the amount of restocking and I'm hugely impressed all this is happening just a year later.

It may have been hard for many locals to accept compliments from someone they had been so critical of. Nonetheless, Finnie was expressing a sentiment that anyone in the area would have echoed. It would have been easy to lie down and admit defeat after the devastation of 2001. Instead, people just got on with their lives while never losing sight of what had happened in the past.

Indeed, although the disease has not returned the aftermath is still being felt today and is likely to continue for some time. The announcement in May 2004 that the government would consider the use of vaccinations in any future crisis must have brought a bitter smile to many in Dumfries and Galloway. While the move was welcomed it had come too late for many who questioned both the cull and the pre-emptive cull policy three years earlier. The vice-president of the National Farmers Union of Scotland, David Mitchell, said:

> There are many lessons to be learned from the 2001 outbreak. The industry will be reassured that the Executive is taking on board the recommendations of the FMD inquiries and a robust contingency plan is being put in place. In the event of a future outbreak, we must have as many tools as possible at our disposal.

It is sad that it took a disaster of these proportions for this lesson to be learned. Dumfries had been at the heart of a brutal battle against a dreadful disease. Once again the town, and all the surrounding communities, had shown the character that makes it such a special place to live.